AMERICAN EDUCATION

Its Men,

Ideas

and

Institutions

Advisory Editor

Lawrence A. Cremin
Frederick A. P. Barnard Professor of Education
Teachers College, Columbia University

History
of the
Pestalozzian Movement
in the United States

Will S. Monroe

ARNO PRESS & THE NEW YORK TIMES
New York ∗ *1969*

Reprint edition 1969 by Arno Press, Inc.

*

Library of Congress Catalog Card No. 70-89206

*

Reprinted from a copy in Teachers College Library

*

Manufactured in the United States of America

Editorial Note

AMERICAN EDUCATION: *Its Men, Ideas and Institutions* presents selected works of thought and scholarship that have long been out of print or otherwise unavailable. Inevitably, such works will include particular ideas and doctrines that have been outmoded or superseded by more recent research. Nevertheless, all retain their place in the literature, having influenced educational thought and practice in their own time and having provided the basis for subsequent scholarship.

Lawrence A. Cremin
Teachers College

History
of the
Pestalozzian Movement
in the United States

Wm Maclure

History of the
PESTALOZZIAN MOVEMENT

IN

the United States

With nine portraits and a bibliography

BY

WILL S. MONROE

SYRACUSE, N. Y.
C. W. BARDEEN, PUBLISHER

BOOKS BY THE SAME AUTHOR.

1. THE EDUCATIONAL LABORS OF HENRY BARNARD: A Study in the History of American Pedagogy. Syracuse: C. W. Bardeen, 1893. pp. 35. With our portraits and a bibliography.

2. COMENIUS' SCHOOL OF INFANCY: An Essay on the Education of Youth during the First Six Years. (Heath's Pedagogical Library.) Edited with notes, introduction, bibliography, and portrait of Comenius. Boston: D. C. Heath and Company. London: Isbister and Company, 1896. pp. xiv plus 99.

3. BIBLIOGRAPHY OF EDUCATION. (International Education Series.) New York: D. Appleton and Company. 1897. pp. xxiv plus 202.

4. DIE ENTWICKELUNG DES SOZIALEN BEWUSSTSEINS DER KINDER: Studie zur Psychologie und Paedagogik der Kindheit. (Sammlung von Abhandlungen aus dem Gebiete der paedagogischen Psychologie und Physiologie.) Berlin: Reuther und Reichard. 1899. pp. 88.

5. The same translated into Swedish by J. Engdhal. Lund: Ph. Lindstedt, 1900.

6. The same translated into Dutch by M. J. Vles. Amsterdam: G. P. Tierie, 1904.

7. COMENIUS AND THE BEGINNINGS OF EDUCATIONAL REFORM. (Great Educator Series.) New York: Charles Scribner's Sons. London: William Heinemann 1900. pp. xi plus 184.

To

my Teacher and Friend

PROFESSOR EARL BARNES

this volume is dedicated with the warm esteem

and the high regard of

The Author

PREFACE

No educator in modern times has more profoundly influenced his contemporaries and immediate successors than Pestalozzi. More marked in Germany than elsewhere, the United States, nevertheless, felt the impulse of the new movement; and at an early period American students of education visited Yverdon and brought to the new world the message of the Swiss reformer.

The history of education in the United States is unfortunately yet unwritten; and young as our country is in years, many of the men and movements connected with its beginnings are already forgotten, or remembered only by a few special students. This is true in a marked degree of the early American disciples of Pestalozzi.

The purpose of the present work is to trace this movement in the United States, and to place on record the labors of a score of men who caught something of Pestalozzi's insight and

1

enthusiasm and who sought to bring about a better order in the educational world by the adaptation of his reforms to the conditions in the new world.

A brief survey of the European movement seemed needful since many Americans were directly influenced by German and English disciples. A chapter is given to Mr. William Maclure, an American by adoption and a philanthropist by profession. His contribution to the Pestalozzian movement was early and large; and yet it is more than probable that scarcely a score of our professional educators of to-day know more than his name.

The name of Joseph Neef and the title of his excellent book are scarcely better known than Mr. Maclure's labors; and yet it was Neef who published the first book on the science of education in the new world. Three chapters are devoted to Neef—one to his life, another to an analysis of his educational writings, and a third to his first efforts to introduce Pestalozzi's method in American education.

The educational feature of Owen's social experiments at New Harmony, in the sixth chapter, continues the labors of Maclure and Neef and introduces a half dozen scientists and reformers vaguely interested in the general Pestalozzian movement.

While many New England educational reformers became ardent advocates of the doctrines of Pestalozzi, the seventh chapter points out that this section of the United States was less profoundly influenced by the new doctrines than other parts of the country.

The Oswego movement, while of later origin, for a period of twenty years or more made generally familiar to the American educational public the system of Pestalozzi, and more particularly his use of object teaching; and still later the public schools of St. Louis, under the judicious superintendency of William T. Harris, applied the same feature of Pestalozzi's scheme to the teaching of natural science in the elementary schools.

A brief chapter traces the publication of the

writings of Pestalozzi in this country and the exposition of his doctrines by American disciples; and there has been appended a bibliography, to which the small numbers in the body of the book refer.

The author wishes to express his sense of obligation to numerous friends who have aided him in his work. To Professor Earl Barnes he is indebted for the use of considerable material relating to Joseph Neef; and to the late Mrs. Robert Owen, Mr. Neef's daughter, for the use of many of the papers and documents belonging to and relating to her father. Professor Amos W. Farnham has aided in verifying several of the dates in the chapter on the Oswego movement and furnished two portraits. Bibliographic references, in the closing chapter, indicate the authorities consulted in the preparation of the book. For the use of many of these books, the author is indebted to that splendid literary workshop, the City Library at Springfield, Massachusetts.

A portrait of Joseph Neef is published for the

first time; and the portraits of William Maclure and William C. Woodbridge are published for the second time from works that have long been out of print. Mr. Frank B. Sanborn and Little, Brown & Co. kindly permitted the use of the portrait of A. Bronson Alcott.

WILL S. MONROE

Westfield, Mass., December the 16th, 1906

CONTENTS

LIST OF PORTRAITS.

CHAPTER I

Spread of Pestalozzianism in Europe

Widespread dissemination of the doctrines of Pestalozzi. Influence in Switzerland: Fellenberg and Wehrli.—Krüsi, Tobler, Nägeli and de Guimps. Influence in Germany: Fichte—Grüner—Froebel — Herbart—Ritter—von Turk—Harnisch — Plamann — Denzel—Zeller—Blochmann—Diesterweg. Influence in France: Jullien, Chavannes and de Biran. Influence in Spain: Voitel and William Maclure. Influence in Russia and Denmark. Influence in England: Greaves — Charles and Elizabeth Mayo — Home and Colonial School Society.

It is not the purpose of the present work to define Pestalozzianism or to discuss the principles upon which it is based. Such definitions and discussions will be found in the standard works treating of the subject by Barnard,[2] de Guimps,[5] Krüsi[8] and Pinloche[13]; and bibliographic references to these works will be found at the end of this volume. The purpose

9

of the author, on the other hand, is to trace the
diffusion of Pestalozzianism, first, briefly in the
countries of Europe, and, secondly, in much
more detail, in the United States.

The doctrines of no other great educational
reformer have received such wide dissemination
and such general acceptance as those of Pestalozzi; and it is of interest to the student of
education to know the agencies operating in
this dispersion and adoption. Not only Switzerland, but Germany, France, Spain, Russia,
Denmark, England and the United States made
immediate application of the chief reforms advocated by Pestalozzi.

1. *Switzerland*

Pestalozzi was not without honor in his own
country. Indeed, as Krüsi[8] has pointed out,
Switzerland was the first country to adopt his
methods and to profit by the principles which he
established. A less formidable list of Pestalozzian disciples is presented to the historian of ed-

ucation by Switzerland than by Germany; nevertheless, there are worthy and distinguished names on the list—including Fellenberg, Wehrli, Krüsi, Tobler, Nabholz, de Guimps, and Nägeli.

Philipp Emmanuel von Fellenberg (1771-1844), the founder of a famous school on Pestalozzian lines at Hofwyl, attained a larger measure of material success than his master. Twice (1804 and again in 1817) Pestalozzi associated himself with Fellenberg, but they found it impossible to agree. The school at Hofwyl was organized in 1799 and during the first half of the last century it was the most successful and—to except Yverdon—the most famous educational institution in Europe. It consisted of a group of educational institutions, including a farm of six hundred acres, workshops for the manufacture and repair of clothing and agricultural implements, a printing establishment, a literary institution for the education of the sons of the better classes, a trade school, an agricultural school. Fellenberg had philanthropic motives—receiving poor boys and even convicts

—but he endeavored to make his school self-supporting. He also provided special courses of pedagogic instruction for Swiss teachers. He entirely agreed with Pestalozzi that all forms of educational work should be in the nature of recreation. Mr. William Maclure, an American philanthropist, who visited Hofwyl several times during the early years of the last century, wrote: "In thus joining mental with corporeal labor, the Pestalozzian system [at Hofwyl] has a great advantage in all schools of industry; for it not only produces both knowledge and property at the same time, but gives a habit of working and thinking conjointly." The fame of Fellenberg's institution was in no small measure due to Johann Jacob Wehrli(1790-1855), who had been trained under Pestalozzi and who directed at Hofwyl for twenty-three years the educational work of the orphan and destitute children.

Hermann Krüsi, Sr., (1775-1844), after eighteen years of valuable service as Pestalozzi's associate at Burgdorf and Yverdon, was forced to leave the institution. "With a bleeding heart," writes von Raumer," he sent his resignation to Pestalozzi, whom even in his error he loved and respected." In accepting the resignation Pestalozzi wrote him: "With sorrow I see a connection dissolved, which I would willingly have continued until my death, had it been possible." After leaving the institute he conducted for five years a private school at Yverdon which met with a large measure of success and was patronized by many foreign students. In 1822 he accepted the principalship of a cantonal school at Trogan. In 1833 he was selected principal of the normal school at Gais, where, as he says, he was able "to carry out Pestalozzi's system of elementary education, freely and without hindrance."[9] He continued at the head of the normal school at Gais until his death in 1844. Gustav Tobler (1769-1843),who developed the Pestalozzian system of geographic instruction at Burgdorf and Yverdon, continued his labors, after leaving Pestalozzi, at Glarus, Mülhausen, and St. Gallen.

Hans George Nägeli (1773-1836) developed the Pestalozzian method of instruction in music; and, as will be later seen, he influenced profoundly two American music educators, William C. Woodbridge and Lowell Mason. His *Theory of instruction in singing based on Pestalozzian principles*, and published in 1810, was the first successful attempt to place the study of music on a distinctly pedagogical basis. Roger de Guimps (1802-1894), who became the well-known biographer of Pestalozzi; Nabholz, who became principal of a normal school at Aaran, and others associated with the reformer, continued to carry on his work in various parts of Switzerland.

2. *Germany.*

It was in Germany, however, that the doctrines of Pestalozzi earliest found most general acceptance. Crushed and dismembered by the losses following in the train of the battle of Jena, Germany was determined to recover her lost power and to regain her fallen glory by a wise system of public elementary education; and the doctrines of Pestalozzi were accepted as the basis of the reform movements. Young men flocked to Yverdon from Prussia, Saxony and Württemberg in great numbers, and the different German states vied with one another in the ardor of their advocacy of the Swiss reformer's cause. Nearly every really great German educator during the first half of the last century could rightfully lay claim to personal relations with Pestalozzi. The German list is a long one—Fichte, Grüner, Fröbel, Herbart, Ritter, von Türk, Harnisch, Zeller, Ramsauer, Plamann, Denzel, Dinter, Blochmann, Steiner, Hennig, Müller, and Diesterweg, to mention but a few of the best known German Pestalozzian disciples.

John George Fichte (1762-1842) had married a friend of Mrs. Pestalozzi and the two philosophers early became intimately identified in their educational interests; and, while Fichte's doctrines of state education are essentially those of Pestalozzi, we are told by Roger de Guimps that

Pestalozzi's political essays—and notably his *Researches into the course of nature in the development of the human race*—represent the viewpoint of Fichte. As early as 1793 Fichte had visited Pestalozzi, and in his historic addresses to the German people in 1807 and 1808, after the terrible desolations of the Napoleonic wars, he told his countrymen that the only way to raise the people was by education; and if such education was to be effectual and salutary, he declared, they must look to Pestalozzi for reforms in all matters of public instruction.

Dr. Grüner of Frankfort was one of the earliest German schoolmasters to make practical application of Pestalozzi's views; and his school became the centre of interest for the new movement. It was Grüner who first directed Fröbel's attention to the work of education. In the summer of 1805 Friedrich Fröbel (1782-1852), it will be remembered, went to Frankfort for the purpose of engaging in the occupation of architecture. He had been in the city but a few weeks when he met the enthusiastic principal of the new Pestalozzian normal school. Grüner soon convinced the young man that he could do more for the culture and ennobling of men by becoming a teacher than he could possibly do as an architect. Fröbel was soon convinced; and in August he repaired to Yverdon to spend a fortnight with Pestalozzi prior to taking up his new duties as a teacher in Grüner's school. Convinced that teaching was to be his life vocation, he returned to Yverdon again in 1808 and spent two years in study with Pestalozzi. Fröbel tells us that during this period he was both teacher and pupil; and that it was while there that he first recognized the true educational value of play. It need only be mentioned in this connection that most of the great movements associated with the name and fame of Fröbel were movements that, in one form or another, had previously been associated with the institute at Yverdon.

Johann Friedrich Herbart (1776-1841), after he left the university at Jena, began his career as a private tutor in 1797; and, like so many other young German teachers, he was at once attracted to Burgdorf, where Pestalozzi was teaching at the time. In an able article in the *Educational Review* on Herbart and Pestalozzi compared, William T. Harris calls attention to the fact that "the progress of education is a zigzag line, from extreme to extreme. * * * At one time the schools have tended almost exclusively to memory culture, with very little attempt at verification by original research and observation. This was the case with what was called the old education. * *

* But Pestalozzi exploded the theory on which it rests and substituted another. He laid stress on sense-perception, verification, and original research. The practice of our time may not correspond to its theory, but certainly all writers uphold the Pestalozzian doctrines of instruction by object lessons. But while this reform is progressing toward its extreme, another tendency has begun within a few years, and it promises to force a new departure on our zigzag line. This

is the doctrine of Herbart, which holds that it is not so much sense-perception that is wanted in education as apperception—not so much seeing and hearing and handling things, as recognizing and understanding them.''

Karl Ritter (1779-1859), the great German geographer, tells us that it was from Pestalozzi that he learned the pedagogic principles of his science. ''Pestalozzi did not know as much geography as a child in our primary schools,'' wrote Ritter, ''but, none the less, I learned the science of geography from him; for it was in listening to him that there first awakened in me the idea of a natural method. He showed me the way.'' While a private tutor at Frankfort, after having finished his university studies at Halle, Ritter came in contact with the group of Pestalozzian disciples whom Grüner had reared up; and he became so deeply interested in the new educational movement that he repaired to Yverdon in 1807. He tells us that he was filled with admiration and respect in the presence of a man like

Pestalozzi, devoted to one grand, original idea, yet his was a nature in which simplicity and humility were united with boundless confidence in the greatness of his task.   He says he left Yverdon full of what he had learned there and feeling that he had entered a new world, enriched and ennobled beyond all conception.   He visited Yverdon again in 1809 and wrote: "The good old Pestalozzi remains still young in heart and full of the spirit of fire and restlessness."   Hennig, who later became distinguished in German geography in the matter of Heimatskunde (home geography), also passed some years at Yverdon as one of the pupil-teachers sent there by the German government; and it was while there that he learned the method which he afterwards developed, of teaching geography to beginners in the open air and without the use of books.

Karl Christian Wilhelm von Türk (1774-1846), who was of noble family and who resigned a judgeship to learn the teacher's art with Pestalozzi, devoted his life to the education and care of poor children. Horace Mann (1796-1859), who visited him in 1843, wrote: "At the head of the private orphan asylum in Potsdam is the venerable von Türk. According to the laws of the country he is a nobleman. His talents and acquisitions were such, that, at a very early age, he was elevated to the bench. He officiated as judge for fourteen years; but in the course o time, so many criminal cases were brought before him for adjudication, whose only origin was so plainly referable to early neglect in the culprit's education, that the noble heart of the judge could no longer bear to pronounce sentence of condemnation against the prisoners, for he looked upon them as men, who, almost without a paradox, might be called guiltless offenders. While holding the office of judge, he was appointed school inspector. The paramount importance of the latter office grew upon his mind, as he executed his duties, until at last he came to the full conception of the grand and sacred truth—how much more intrinsically honorable is the vocation of the teacher, who saves from crime and wrong, than that of the magistrate, who waits till they are committed and then avenges them. He immediately resigned his office as judge, with its life tenure and salary; travelled to Switzerland where he placed himself under the care of Pestalozzi; and after availing himself for three years of the instruction of that celebrated teacher, he returned to take charge of an orphan asylum. Since that time he has devoted his whole life to the care of the neglected and destitute." Aside from his noble example and the free expenditure of his own private fortune for the education of needy children, von Türk published numerous writings on the Pestalozzian system; and during September 1816 he gave a course of lectures upon Pestalozzi's method to sixty clergymen and school teachers at Frankfort on the Oder.

Wilhelm Harnisch (1787-1864) studied the Pestalozzian system with Plamann in Berlin and introduced the system into the normal school at Breslau and later in the normal school at Weissenfels, which, as Americans will recall, is the institution which Horace Mann, Alexander Dallas Bache and Calvin E. Stowe praised so heartily in their reports of European schools. Johannes Ramsauer (1790-1848) received his elementary and secondary education under Pestalozzi and Krüsi at Burgdorf and Yverdon, and in the latter institution he served as pupil-teacher for some years. In 1816 he became a teacher in a Pestalozzian school at Würzburg and later in a similar school at Stuttgart. He popularized in Germany Pestalozzi's methods of teaching drawing and form (elementary geometry).

Johann Ernst Plamann (1771-1834), after Grüner, was one of the earliest ardent advocates of Pestalozzianism in Germany. He spent some time with the master at Burgdorf during the early days of that institution and he established and maintained in Berlin for many years one of the best known educational institutions in Germany. He published many works on the methods and doctrines of Pestalozzi and he won many converts

for the new system. Bernard Gottlieb Denzel
(1773-1838) was the most influential promoter of
Pestalozzianism in the kingdom of Würtemberg.
He spent some time at both Burgdorf and Yverdon; and, while deeply in earnest himself, he had
a conciliatory manner—and, more important
still, he had the confidence of the clergy, so that
progress in educational reform was both rapid and
permanent. For many years he was principal of
the normal school at Esslingen which was founded
on Pestalozzian principles. Karl August Zeller
(1774-1847) as early as 1804 established a charity
school at Tübingen for the purpose of trying Pestalozzi's plans for regenerating the poor. Later
he became identified with the movement of establishing a training school for teachers at Zurich.
After nearly two years in Switzerland he returned
to Germany in 1809 and organized an orphan school
at Königsberg and a normal and model school
as a feature of the same. By May 1810 the lectures on Pestalozzi's methods and doctrines at
this school were attended by one hundred and

four teachers, pastors and school superintendents; and a year later he was asked to organize a second similar institution at Braunsberg. His last establishment was the well known Pestalozzian institution at Lichtenstein. Raumer says of him: "He was energetic not only in introducing new discoveries [of Pestalozzi] in pedagogical science, but also in independently sifting and ingeniously improving its principles already accepted."

Karl Justus Blochmann (1786-1855), who was some time associated with Pestalozzi at Yverdon, afterwards opened a Pestalozzian school at Dresden and later became minister of public instruction in Saxony, a kingdom in which elementary education has always been wisely directed and whose schools are still essentially Pestalozzian. Gustav Friedrich Dinter (1760-1831), while never brought into personal relations with Pestalozzi, in his capacity as school counsellor in Königsberg, he was hearty in his support and advocacy of the Swiss reformer's doctrines. Steiner, who was one of the assistant teachers at Yverdon, became professor of mathematics in the university of Berlin and he wrote several works which aided in rendering Pestalozzi's labors fruitful in Germany.

One of the most influential of the later German Pestalozzians was Friedrich Adolph Wilhelm Diesterweg (1790-1866), who, like so many of his colleagues, acquired his interest in the new movement during his teaching career at Frankfort (1813-1818). He was teacher and acting principal in the normal school at Meurs for twelve years and in 1832 he was called to the principalship of the Berlin normal school where he inaugurated most sweeping reforms. He was instrumental in inaugurating and carrying out so successfully the great Pestalozzi centennial in Germany in 1846 and in the foundation of an institution for orphans as an appropriate monument to the great apostle of the poor and the unfortunate. Barnard very appropriately calls him the most eminent educator and the most efficient promoter in Germany of the principles of Pestalozzi.

Germany was truly fertile soil for the educational ideals which originated at Burgdorf and Yverdon; and as Mr. Pinloche has well remarked: "It was in Germany that Pestalozzi's ideas had the most rapid and wide influence and the best application." And Krüsi remarks in this connection: "By these means the schools of Germany were speedily organized on a new basis, and the thrill of a new, vigorous life was felt from one extremity of the land to the other." In a word, it was in essence the spirit and the method of Pestalozzi which formed the basis of the elementary school renaissance in Germany during the first half of the last century; and Germany regained her losses at Jena through a wise and efficient system of common education.

3. *France and Spain*

Napoleon had no time to occupy himself with A B C's, in consequence of which France profited much less by Pestalozzi's beneficent educational reforms than her neighbor on the other side of the Rhine; and Sedan was the logical outcome, less than three quarters of a century later. A few public spirited gentlemen in France, however, interested themselves in Pestalozzi's doctrines; and endeavored to interest their country, among whom were Jullien, Chavannes, and Maine de Biran. Jullien was a Knight of the Legion of Honor, a member of several learned societies and a man of wealth and influence. He placed his son under Pestalozzi's tuition and induced some of his distinguished friends to do likewise. He published several important works on Pestalozzi's institute and doctrines and aroused more or less interest in the labors of the Swiss reformer. Chavannes placed his daughter in the girls' department of the institute and published a favorable exposition of the institute at Yverdon in 1805 which was widely translated. Maine de Biran, the philosopher, opened a Pestalozzian school at Bergerac, his native town, in 1808, and the school continued in existence for nearly seventy years.

In Spain a Pestalozzian school was opened at

Madrid by Voitel in 1805 and a military institute a year later with the aid of two associate teachers sent from Yverdon; but political events caused the suppression of these schools in 1808. In 1819 Mr. William Maclure, an American disciple of Pestalozzi, founded an agricultural school near the city of Alicante, on a tract of ten thousand acres which he had purchased for the purpose from the Spanish government. But the property was subsequently confiscated and the educational experiment brought to an end in 1824.

4. *Russia and Denmark*

Both Russia and Denmark profited by the reforms of Pestalozzi. The Emperor Alexander had visited Pestalozzi and was so much impressed by his system that he asked that one of his disciples be sent to St. Petersburg for the head of a Pestalozzian institute for the higher classes. Muralt, who had taught French for several years at Yverdon, was selected; and he was eminently successful during his long career at St. Petersburg.

The Danish government in 1803 sent two teachers, Ström and Torlitz, to Burgdorf to study the Pestalozzian system. Upon their return to Copenhagen Pestalozzian institutes were organized with indifferent success.

5. *England*

England did not share with Switzerland and Germany their profound interest in the reforms of Pestalozzi. The English people, as a class, have never concerned themselves very seriously with the study of education as a science; hence, the innovations of Pestalozzi, or of any other great reformer, for that matter, would not be calculated to arouse much interest. Two Englishmen, however, became interested in the work of the Swiss reformer during his closing years; and, at a later period, much that was called Pestalozzian, but which, as Krüsi has pointed out, lacked entirely the true spirit, was current in England during the third and fourth decades of the past century.

James Pierrepont Greaves (1777-1842) had
been a wealthy English merchant; but he lost his
property by French spoliations in Napoleon's
time. Ralph Waldo Emerson, in a sketch of
Greaves in the *Dial*, says: "Quitting business, he
travelled and resided in Germany for some time.
His leisure was given to books of the deepest
character; and in Switzerland he found a brother
in Pestalozzi. With him he remained ten years,
living abstemiously, almost on biscuit and water
and, although they never learned each other's
language, their daily intercourse appears to have
been of the deepest and happiest kind. Mr.
Greaves there [at Yverdon] made himself useful
in a variety of ways. Pestalozzi declared that
Mr. Greaves understood his aim and methods
better than any other observer. And he there
became acquainted with some eminent persons.
Mr. Greaves on his return to England, introduced
as much as he could of the method and life whose
beautiful and successful operations he had wit-
nessed; and although almost all that he did was

misunderstood or dragged downwards, he has been a chief instrument in the regeneration of British schools."

It will be recalled that in 1818 Pestalozzi opened a school for poor children of both sexes at Clendy, a little hamlet near Yverdon; and, in spite of his seventy-two years, he devoted himself to this orphanage with the zeal and enthusiasm of his younger days at Neuhof and Stanz. He was ably supported in this undertaking by Greaves, who taught the poor children without any remuneration. But the school was in existence little more than a year. Vulliemin, in speaking of the Clendy enterprise, says: "There was a man there who had taken part in the short-lived enterprise, a man of Christian spirit and enlightened understanding. This man, who was an Englishman, by name Greaves, carried the ideas he had gathered at Clendy back to England, where they took root, and became the origin of infant schools."

After his return to England in 1825 Greaves became secretary of the Infant School Society in

London. At his request Pestalozzi wrote him a series of thirty-four letters on the education of the child, which he permitted Greaves to translate into English. The English edition appeared in 1827 and three years later the same was republished in Boston. In 1832 he settled in the village of Randwick, Gloucestershire, and engaged in an industrial scheme for the benefit of agricultural laborers; and in 1837 he founded at Ham, near London, a Pestalozzian school which he named Alcott House in honor of the American Pestalozzian, A. Bronson Alcott, whose Cheshire and Boston schools had interested him greatly. He shared Alcott's transcendental views; and a long correspondence ensued between the two philosophers. From all that one can learn concerning Greaves, it seems pretty certain that he understood Pestalozzi well. The careful and sympathetic translation of the *Letters on the early education of the child** would abundantly sustain this

*Mr. C. W. Bardeen, of Syracuse, New York, who has published most of the best American books on Pestalozzi, has lately brought out a well-edited edition of these valuable letters.

point, if other evidence should be lacking; but he seems to have been altogether too serene and thoughtful and benevolent to have influenced his country profoundly, and this was unfortunate for his country.

A very different sort of a man was Charles Mayo (1792-1846), who seems to have caught most of the formalism and little of the spirit of Pestalozzi's benevolent educational doctrines. After concluding his academic training at Merchant Taylor's School and St. John's College, Oxford, he was headmaster of a grammar school at Berdgnorth for two years. While here, one Mr. Synge of Glanmore Castle, Wicklow, interested him in Pestalozzi; and in 1819, with several English pupils, he went to Yverdon where he passed nearly three years. Returning to England in April 1822, he opened a Pestalozzian school for boys of the upper classes at Epsom; and, as his school grew in popularity, he moved it after a few years to Cheam where he continued to conduct it until the time of his death. In 1826 he gave a course of lectures before the Royal Institution on Pestalozzi and his doctrines. He took an active interest in the establishment of the Home and Colonial Training College at Gray's Inn Road, London, which aimed to train teachers in the Pestalozzian methods. He published a memoir of Pestalozzi and several Pestalozzian text-books. Reiner, who held a subordinate place at Yverdon during the declining years of the institute, was for many years in charge of the department of mathematics at Mayo's school. Herman Krüsi, Jr., also taught at Cheam for five years before coming to America.

Mr. Mayo's sister Miss Elizabeth Mayo (1793 -1865) was for many years an instructor in her brother's schools at Epsom and Cheam where she assisted him in applying the doctrines and methods of Pestalozzi. In 1843, when the Home and Colonial Training College was opened at Gray's Inn Road, London, Miss Mayo became superintendent of the institution and served as critic teacher. "The acquisition of Miss Mayo," notes Gill, [4] "gave a decided direction in the system of training adopted to Pestalozzianism." Miss Mayo prepared several works on object teaching, a work on religious instruction, and model lessons for infant schools. "Having adopted Pestalozzianism as its basis," writes a historian of the Home and School Society, "this society's great service to the cause of infant education was the reduction of its principles and methods to a practicable shape. This it did by the preparation of graduated courses of instruction." It was thus that Pestalozzianism was "misunderstood and dragged downward," to borrow Emerson's words. Pestalozzi taught without books, and chiefly in the open air; and the moment the English attempted "to reduce his principles and methods to practicable shape," in the preparation of manuals *about* objects, which manuals were to be studied and the lessons on the objects learned and said to the teachers, that moment a wide gulf separated the Pestalozzianism of Switzerland and Krüsi, Maclure, Neef and Greaves from the Pestaloz-

zianism of England and Mayo, Stowe, and Du-
ning.

These are some of the men and movements in
Europe directly influenced by Pestalozzi and his
reforms. In subsequent chapters similar influences in America will be traced; for the new world,
no less than the old, was profoundly influenced by
the teachings of the educational seer at Yverdon.
William Maclure and Joseph Neef were so influenced; and in lesser degrees John Griscom and
William C. Woodbridge, who also came in personal
relation with Pestalozzi and who brought the
new doctrines to the United States, at an early
period.

CHAPTER II

WILLIAM MACLURE: FIRST AMERICAN DISCIPLE OF PESTALOZZI

Mr. Maclure's birth and early training. Business career. Visit
to the United States. Member of a commission selected
by President Jefferson. Travels in Europe. Visit to
Pestalozzi at Yverdon. Pestalozzi and Fellenberg con-
trasted. Secures services of Joseph Neef for the United
States. Organizes the first geological survey in America.
Connection with the Philadelphia Academy of Natural
Sciences. Educational experiments in Spain. Connect-
tion with the New Harmony community. Industrial
school experiment. Closing years in Mexico. Benefactions. His character and influence.

Philadelphia, through the efforts of one of her
public spirited citizens, was the first city in the
new world to recognize the merit of Pestalozzi's
great educational reforms, and to give these reforms practical application on this side of the
Atlantic. The first disciple of the Swiss re-

former in the United States was an adopted son of the Quaker City, who not only familiarized his countrymen with the teachings of Pestalozzi, but who brought to America, at his own expense, one of Pestalozzi's associates from Burgdorf.

This disciple was William Maclure. Mr. Maclure was born at Ayr, Scotland, March 22, 1763, and received an elementary education in the English branches, mathematics and the ancient languages. Maclure's teacher said of him that while he mastered the several branches of study it was observed at an early period that he was disposed to reject the learning of the schools for the simpler and more attractive truths of natural history. He engaged in commercial pursuits; and at the early age of nineteen he made a business trip to the United States in the interest of the London firm of Miller, Hart & Co. He subsequently became a member of the firm; and in 1796 he again visited the United States to arrange some unsettled business connected with his establishment. He became deeply interested in the civic and social problems of the young republic and returned to London with the determination of ultimately making his permanent home in Philadelphia. By 1803 he had devoted himself to business with such assiduity that his rewards justified his retirement, and he decided to remove to the new world and consecrate the remainder of his life to public service.

His first public service was as a member of the commission selected by the United States to settle the claims of American citizens against the French government for spoliations committed during the revolution in that country. He displayed marked ability and great diligence on this commission and accomplished the object of his appointment to the general satisfaction of the American government. In connection with his labors on this commission, he devoted his spare moments while in Europe to the collection of objects for a museum of natural history for the United States and to a study of the systems of popular education in the old world. To accomplish the first object he traversed the most interesting portions of Europe, from the Mediterranean sea to the Baltic and from the British Isles to Bohemia. During his travels he became greatly interested in the study of geology and he determined upon his return to commence a geological survey of the United States.

Pestalozzi and Fellenberg were at this time the commanding figures in European education, and Mr. Maclure visited the institutions at Yverdon*

*Yverdon is a town of 6000 inhabitants at the foot of lake Neuchatel in the canton of Vaud. Here in a large stone castle Pestalozzi for twenty years (1805–1825) conducted his famous educational institute. It was a rather complex establishment, including an infant department, composed chiefly of orphans, a secondary (boarding) school for boys, a normal school for young men, and a pedagogical seminary for trained and experienced teachers. During the years of its greatest prosperity (1805–1817) it was visited by most of the noted educators of Europe and America and by many European rulers, including the czar of Russia and the kings of Spain, Holland, Prussia, Denmark, Würtemberg, and Saxony. Among distinguished publicists, besides Mr. Maclure, who visited Pestalozzi at Yverdon, may be named Thaddeus Kosciusko, the Polish patriot who fought with

and Hofwyl. He was keenly interested in the agricultural phases of Fellenberg's school and he praised heartily Fellenberg's efforts to make the school self-supporting and to cause instruction to be regarded by the pupils as a recreation. He was struck by the cheerfulness and eagerness to learn which was shown by the pupils, many of whom came from poor families and some of them were the offspring of convicts. But Mr. Maclure did not find the democratic atmosphere at Hofwyl, which he regarded as so essential in the up-building of a system of popular education. Fellenberg was descended from a noble family; he had held important state offices before the organization of his school, and he ruled the institution at Hofwyl in a dictatorial manner.

Pestalozzi, on the other hand, was the essence of democracy, and Mr. Maclure was delighted with the spirit of co-operation and fraternity

Lafayette in the American Revolution; Count Zinzendorf, the the Austrian minister of finance; and Prince Esterhazy, the Hungarian statesman.

which characterized the institution at Yverdon.
He visited Pestalozzi in 1804 and again in 1805.
During the latter visit he endeavored to secure
the services of Pestalozzi for a new institution
which he proposed to establish in Philadelphia.
But the Swiss reformer was already in his six-
tieth year; and, unfamiliar as he was with the
English language, he was not able to accept Mr.
Maclure's proposition.   He heartily commended
to Mr. Maclure's favorable consideration one of
his former associate teachers at Burgdorf, one
Joseph Neef, at the time in charge of a Pestalozzian school in Paris. Maclure repaired to Paris,
visited Neef's school, and engaged his services.
An account of the engagement and labors of
Neef will be given in the next chapter.

The late Henry Barnard[1] is authority for the
statement that the earliest presentation of the
principles of Pestalozzi to the people of the United
States came from Mr. Maclure in an article in the
National Intelligencer printed in Washington on
the sixth of June in the year 1806. This was

followed on the ninth and thirtieth of the same month by elaborate expositions of Pestalozzi's method taken from the French work by D. A. Chavannes published in Paris the previous year, and subsequently translated into the Italian and Spanish languages.

Upon his return to the United States in 1806, Mr. Maclure began, and for three years he studiously pursued, one of the objects of his ambition, which he had long contemplated, viz., a geological survey of the United States. One of his biographers says of this labor of scientific love: "In this extraordinary undertaking we have a forcible example of what individual effort can accomplish, unsustained by government patronage and unassisted by collateral aids. At a time when scientific pursuits were little known and still less appreciated in this country, he commenced his herculean task. He went forth with his hammer in his hand and his wallet on his shoulder, pursuing his researches in every direction, often amid pathless tracts and dreary solitudes until he had crossed and re-crossed the Alleghany mountains no less than fifty times. He encountered all the privations of hunger, thirst, fatigue, and exposure, month after month, year after year, until his indomitable spirit had conquered every difficulty and crowned his enterprise with success." He visited every state and territory in the union from the St. Lawrence to the Gulf of Mexico; and in 1809 he presented the results of his investigations to the American Philosophical Society in Philadelphia. He continued his geological studies for eight years longer and in 1817 he presented to the same society the final revision of his labors, accompanied by a colored map and sections of the survey. The report was published in the society's transactions and as a separate volume. It placed Mr. Maclure among the first of living geologists and stimulated an interest in that sort of scientific research which still continues fruitful in the United States. He was a liberal benefactor of the American Geological Society (of which he was the first president in 1828) and he has been aptly characterized as the father of American geology.

Mr. Maclure did much to develop scientific tastes and talents in Philadelphia and he was the moving spirit of the Academy of Natural Sciences. That institution, it will be recalled, was founded January 1812, by seven men who resolved to meet once each week for the purpose of conversing on scientific subjects and thus communicate to each other the results of their reading, observation and reflection. He was president of the society from 1817 to the time of his death—a period of nearly twenty-three years—and he bequeathed to the society his valuable library and a money gift of twenty thousand dollars.

In 1819 he returned to Europe. He spent some time at New Lanark, Scotland, in studying the industrial and educational schemes of Robert Owen*; he passed some months with distinguished

---

*Robert Owen (1771–1858), the founder of English socialism, was the manager and part owner of the large cotton mills at New Lanark. Of the 2000 people employed as workmen, 500

scientists in Paris where he was already favorably known through French translations of his geological studies; and toward the close of that year he located near the city of Alicante, Spain, where he continued to reside for nearly five years.

His attention was called to Spain as a fertile field for philanthropy by the promulgation by the Spanish Cortes of a liberal constitution which promised a comparatively free government to a country long oppressed by every species of bondage. His plan was the establishment of a great agricultural school, after the manner of Pestalozzi and Fellenberg, in which manual labor should

---

were children, most of whom had been brought from alms houses and orphanages in Edinburgh and Glasgow. Cotton mill operatives represented the lowest of the population of the period, since the English country people would not submit to the long hours and the demoralized conditions of factory life. Owen sought to ameliorate and elevate the social, economic, and intellectual condition of his workmen (1) by the organization of infant schools (the first in England); (2) by strict supervision of the sale of alcoholic drinks; (3) by improved sanitation, and (4) by courses of instruction and training in habits of order, cleanliness, and thrift.

be combined with intellectual studies and moral training. He sought especially to elevate the lower classes and to educate them for self-maintenance and self-government. He purchased from the Cortes a tract of ten thousand acres of land which the government had confiscated from the church. Buildings were repaired, new ones were erected, and the estate was placed in order to carry out his educational scheme; but almost before his institution was well under way, the constitutional government was overthrown; the priests were re-invested in their estate, and Mr. Maclure was dispossessed without ceremony or reimbursement. In a letter to his friend Professor Benjamin Silliman from Alicante under date of March the 6th, 1824 he says: "I have been disappointed in being prevented from executing my mineralogical excursions in Spain by the bands of powerful robbers that have long infested the astonishingly extended surface of uncultivated and inhospitable wilds in this naturally delightful country."

Mr. Maclure returned to the United States in 1824 determined to establish an agricultural school similar to the one he had contemplated in Spain. At this juncture, his friend Robert Owen projected his New Harmony community. Maclure had previously studied Owen's reforms in factory life and his system of infant schools at New Lanark, and he willingly joined the Utopian colony at New Harmony, Indiana. According to Mr. Owen's subsequent statement, Mr. Maclure invested one hundred and fifty thousand dollars in the New Harmony experiment, but his liability in the undertaking was limited to ten thousand dollars. "The avowed intention of Mr. Maclure was to make New Harmony the centre of American education through the introduction of the Pestalozzian system of instruction." To this end he brought to New Harmony a distinguished coterie of educators and scientists, including, besides Joseph Neef, a co-adjutor of Pestalozzi, Thomas Say, the father of American zoölogy, Charles Alexander Lesueur, the distinguished French botanist, Constantine Samuel Rafinesque, whom David Starr Jordan characterizes as "the very first teacher of natural history in the west," Gerard Troost, the Dutch geologist, and Madame Marie D. Frotegeot and Phiquepal d' Arusmont, two Pestalozzian teachers whom Maclure had brought to Philadelphia from Europe. During the two brief years of the existence of the community, Mr. Maclure gave his entire time to the direction of the school and the promotion of scientific studies.

Mr. Maclure contemplated the establishment of an industrial school in New Harmony after the manner of Pestalozzi, concerning which he wrote: "In thus joining mental with corporeal labor, the Pestalozzian system has a great advantage in all schools of industry; for it not only produces both knowledge and property at the same time, but gives habits of working and thinking conjointly, which last during life, and doubles the powers of production, while it alleviates the fatigue of labor by a more agreeable occupation of the mind.''

Mr. Maclure and his friends purchased a tract of one thousand acres and provided suitable buildings for the use of the teachers and work-men connected with the industrial school, as well as for storing grain, and for stables, workshops, schoolrooms, and accommodations for meetings, concerts and recreations. In 1826 he petitioned the Indiana legislature for the incorporation of the institution under the title of the New Har-mony Educational Society, stating that he ''had bought in and about New Harmony one thous-sand acres of land with suitable buildings erected thereupon, devoted to the establishment of schools, and furnished a liberal endowment, em-bracing many thousands of volumes of books, with such mathematical, chemical, and physical apparatus as are necessary to facilitate education.'' Because of the religious bigotry of the Indiana senate, the bill failed by a vote of fifteen to four. In the senate and throughout the state of Indiana the impression prevailed that atheism was promulgated in the New Harmony schools. The religious tolerance of Mr. Maclure and his colleagues, and their opposition to narrow dogmatic and sectarian instruction, formed about the only basis for this impression; for no one familiar with the New Harmony movement could sustain the charge of irreligion against Maclure, Neef and the other educational leaders.

After the failure of the New Harmony community, Mr. Maclure purchased a large tract of land in the vicinity and continued his educational experiments along industrial and agricultural lines. In the prospectus[4] of his school he announced: "Young men and young women are received without any expense to them either for teaching or food, lodging or clothing. Hours from five in the morning until eight in the evening, divided as follows: The scholars rise at five; at half past five each goes to his occupation; at seven the bell rings for breakfast; at eight they return to work; at eleven their lessons begin, continuing until half past two, including half an hour for luncheon, then they return to their occupations until five, when a bell calls them to dinner. Afterwards until half past six they exercise themselves in various ways; then the evening lessons begin and last until eight." A biographer remarks: "The arrangements for training and instructing this interesting family were ample; and there would seem to be no obstacle in the way of a successful experiment, if there had been no radical defect of the principle." For a number of years Mr. Maclure continued to reside at New Harmony, engaged chiefly in scientific and literary labors.

On account of failing health he passed several winters in Mexico and ultimately transferred his residence to San Angel, near the City of Mexico, where he died March the 23d, 1840, in the seventy-seventh year of his age. "Thus" said Samuel G. Morton [6] in an address before the Academy of Natural Sciences of Philadelphia July 1, 1841, "closed a life which had been devoted, with untiring energy and singular disinterested-ness, to the attainment and diffusion of practical knowledge. No views of pecuniary advantage or personal aggrandizement entered into the motives by which he was governed. His educa-tional plans, it is true, were repeatedly inopera-tive, not because he did too little but because he expected more than could be realized in the social institutions by which he was surrounded. He aimed at reforming mankind by diverting their attention from the mere pursuit of wealth and ambition to the cultivation of the mind, and, espousing the hypothesis of the possible 'equality of education, property, and power among men,' he labored to counteract that love of superior-ity which appeared to him to cause half the mis-eries of our species." Mr. Maclure never married but he devoted the fortune that had come to him through more than twenty years of careful application to business to the establishment of a better social order and the dissemination of what he thought to be saner doctrines of life. Of his numerous benefactions to education and science, Professor Benjamin Silliman said: "This gentleman's liberality to purposes of science and humanity has been too often and too munificently experienced in this country to demand any eulogium from me. It is rare that affluence, liberality and the possession and love of science unite so signally in the same individual."

It is well known that Mr. Robert Owen and Mr. Maclure were not in accord concerning the administration of the New Harmony community; but Mr. Owen[7] in his Autobiography pays this tribute to his colleague: "Mr. Maclure was a remarkable instance of devotion to his chosen studies. It would be difficult to name any one to match him in the indefatigable energy with which he pursued his investigations of the phennomena and laws of natural science or of the liberality with which he contributed to its advancement. He was a gentleman of large means, of liberal spirit and without a family."

For a period of nearly thirty-five years Mr.

Maclure championed the doctrines of Pestalozzi in the new world. His essays on education were printed in pamphlet form or in periodicals of a transient nature, so that I have been unable to make anything like a complete bibliography of his writings. I have secured the titles of about thirty educational essays, but the number must have been much greater. In all his writings he alludes in glowing terms to the sanity and efficiency of Pestalozzi's doctrines. In an essay[4] on the *Advantages of the Pestalozzian system of education*, published at New Harmony in 1831, he says: "Having travelled seven summers in Switzerland, and some months of each residing at Pestalozzi's school at Yverdon, I never saw the pupils in or out of school without one of the teachers presiding at their games, all of which were calculated to convey instruction. They were constantly occupied with something useful to themselves or to others, from five o'clock in the morning to eight o'clock at night, with the exception of four half hours at meals at which all the teachers ate with the pupils. Their attention was never fatigued with more than one hour at the same exercise, either moral or physical; all was bottomed on free-will, by the total exclusion of every species of correction. Their actions were cheerful, energetic and rapidly tending towards the end aimed at. I do not recall ever to have heard a cry or any demonstration of pain or displeasure, nor even an angry word from either teacher or pupil all the time that I lived amongst them. Though I often went out of my road fifty leagues to examine young men taught under this system, I do not ever remember finding one of an ill-natured temper, or bad conduct, of all that I saw either in Europe or in this country, and I generally found them greatly superior, in all useful accomplishments, to those educated by other methods. It is on this practical proof of the great superiority of the system that my confidence in its immense utility to mankind has been founded, as I do not pretend to be a judge of scholastic exercises without seeing the result.

"One of the most beneficial consequences is the pleasure all Pestalozzi's pupils take in mental labor and study. Agreeable sensations being connected with intellectual employment from the earliest dawn of reason, it continues to be an ornament throughout life; and all my experience forces me firmly to believe that education may, with great ease and pleasure, be so conducted as to render, by early habits, all the useful and necessary operations of both males and females, a pastime and amusement, converting life itself with a play in spite of the delusion of the imagination."

There is, I think, no doubt but that Mr. Maclure rendered Pestalozzi important financial aid in carrying on his institution at Yverdon. John Griscom[2] in writing of his departure from Pestalozzi at Yverdon October the 10th, 1818 says: "Toward those who have generously contributed to aid him in his pecuniary difficulties his heart

glows with the liveliest gratitude. Of two of
my acquaintances, one in London and the other
in Philadelphia, who have thus befriended him,
he could not speak without emotion." The
Philadelphia acquaintance was undoubtedly the
noble minded and public spirited philanthropist,
William Maclure.

Joseph Neef

CHAPTER III

Joseph Neef: Coadjutor of Pestalozzi

Birth and training of Neef. Connection with Napoleon. Instructor under Pestalozzi at Burgdorf. Organizes a Pestalozzian school in Paris. Character of the Paris school. Employment of Neef by William Maclure. The contract. Teaching at Philadelphia, Village Green, Louisville and New Harmony. Social and personal characteristics.

As suggested in the previous chapter, Mr. William Maclure engaged Joseph Neef, a former colleague of Pestalozzi, to come to the United States to introduce the work of reform so well begun in Europe by the famous Swiss educator. Francis Joseph Nicholas Neef was born at Soultz, Alsace, on the sixth of December in the year 1770. His father was a miller by occupation; and the son was destined for the priesthood and was educated accordingly. But when twenty-one years of age he experienced profound changes in his religious views and he gave up the idea of taking orders and entered the French army under Napoleon. He was severely wounded in the famous battle at Arcole in Italy in 1796 and forced to retire from military service. A bullet had lodged in his head and it continued to cause him pain up to the time of his death.

Quitting the army he turned his attention to education. Pestalozzi's writings had attracted his notice and he had been much inspired by the aims and ideals of the Swiss reformer. When he joined Pestalozzi is nowhere positively stated. In his *Sketch of a plan and method of education*[3] he says: "About a year after Pestalozzi's school was established, I became acquainted with him." The school at Burgdorf was opened in 1799, so that he must have joined Pestalozzi about 1800. He taught music, gymnastics and French at Burgdorf.

*Burgdorf, a town of 7000 inhabitants, on the Emmen river, eleven miles northeast of Bern, was the scene of Pestalozzi's labors from 1799 to 1804. His school included an orphanage and a training school for male teachers. Associated with Pestalozzi at Burgdorf, besides Neef, were Herman Krüsi, Sr., Johannes Niederer, Gustav Tobler, and Johannes Buss.

The character of his teaching is best given by Ramsauer [6] who was a student at Burgdorf at the time. He says: "Our joy reached its climax when our gymnastic master, Neef, with his peculiar charm, took part in it. This Neef was an old soldier who had fought in all parts of the world. He was a giant with a great beard, a crabbed face, a severe air, a rude exterior, but he was kindness itself. When he marched with the air of a trooper at the head of sixty or eighty children, his great voice thundering a Swiss air, then he enchanted the whole school. Singing was always a true means of recreation at Burgdorf. We sang everywhere, in the open air, when travelling, when walking, in the evening in the court of the castle, and this singing together contributed much to keep up a spirit of good feeling and harmony amongst us. I should say that Neef, in spite of the rudeness of his exterior, was the pupils' favorite, and for this reason he lived always with them, and felt happiest when amongst them. He played, exercised, walked, bathed, threw stones with the pupils all in a childish spirit; this is how he had such unlimited authority over them. Meanwhile he was not a pedagogue, he only had the heart of one."

Pestalozzi, having been chosen a member of the Helvetian council, was frequently called to Paris to settle disputes and look after the interests of the Swiss people. The educational doctrines of Pestalozzi had already been made familiar to the French people by Jullien and other French apostles of the Swiss reformer; and a philanthropic society, having in charge the care and training of forty orphans, had requested Pestalozzi to send one of his associates to take charge of the institution and conduct it on Pestalozzian lines. Because of his familiarity with the French language, Neef was sent from Burgdorf to undertake this work. Before his departure for Paris, in July 1803, he married Eloise Buss, the sister of John Buss, one of Pestalozzi's first assistants. Mr. Neef's daughter, Mrs. Richard Owen, under date of January the 1st., 1893, writes me from New

Harmony, Indiana, concerning her mother: "My mother was the only sister of John Buss, who was a professor in Pestalozzi's school at Burgdorf and two of his brothers were there as students. Being greatly pleased with the system of instruction, he was desirous of having his sister educated there also. But the school at Burgdorf admitted only boys. As Madame Pestalozzi had no children she was persuaded to take Eloise under her personal supervision. She went to Pestalozzi's school at the age of fifteen and remained until her marriage at the age of eighteen, receiving all her instruction in the form of private lessons." Neef, it should be noted, gave her private lessons in French. Neef and Eloise Buss were married at Burgdorf on the 5th of July 1803, in the presence of Pestalozzi and his wife and the members of the institution. The quaint marriage certificate with the witness signatures of Pestalozzi and his wife was sent me by Mrs. Richard Owen with numerous other documents used in the preparation of this work. Concerning his wife Neef says in his

Sketch:[3] "Mistress Neef, according to what she often tells me, and I of course must believe, is an excellent contriver in housekeeping; she shall therefore be entrusted with the management of our domestic affairs. Like the honest Vicar of Wakefield, I chose my wife, not for a glossy surface, but for such qualities as I thought would wear well."

Concerning the Paris school little can be learned. Neef was there less than three years, and the French were too busy waging wars to give much attention to educational reform. Pompée,[4] in his life of Pestalozzi, published in French in 1850, gives the following account of Neef's school and of a reputed visit to the same made by Napoleon: "Mons. Neef, a teacher of Burgdorf, was sent to Paris and commenced teaching in the orphanage, where the administration of benevolent institutions entrusted a certain number of children to him. Napoleon wishing to see for himself the results of the teaching, went to the orphanage accompanied by Tallyrand, the embassador from the United States, and a number of distinguished people; he left well satisfied with what he saw.   *

*   *   Whilst all the governments of Europe were thinking of introducing a new system of teaching in the elementary schools, a private individual, Mr. Maclure, conferred upon his country, the United States, an establishment that could vie with the most important schools of Europe. A singular chance led him toward the improvement of his country's instruction.   In 1804 he was in Paris and had a great desire to see Napoleon.   He applied to the embassador from the United States who took him to the meeting where Napoleon had gone to see the results of Neef's teaching of the orphans.   During the whole time that the exercises were going on, Maclure, absorbed in looking at Napoleon, saw nothing else; but, on going away, he heard Tallyrand say, 'It is too much for us.'   This remark struck him; he returned to the room and learned from Neef the object of the meeting; and, as he was deeply interested in the improvement of the con-

dition of the poorer classes, he saw at once all that Pestalozzi's system could do to benefit their condition. He made a very favorable offer to Neef to go to Philadelphia, and later on to New Harmony to found a Pestalozzian institute."

The late Roger de Guimps, the most trustworthy biographer of Pestalozzi, gives the above quotation from Pompée "for what it is worth," admitting that it lacks corroboration. The facts of Mr. Maclure's visit to Neef have been given in the second chapter of this work. These facts are from Neef himself and they are probably correct. Concerning his meeting with Mr. Maclure, Neef says in the introduction of his *Sketch of a plan and method of education*: "In the summer of 1805, Mr. William Maclure of Philadelphia, one of Pennsylvania's most enlightened sons, happened to visit Helvetia's interesting mountains and valleys. He was accompanied by C. Cabell, a brother of the present governor of Virginia. Pestalozzi's school attracted their notice. They repaired thither and were soon convinced of the

solidity, importance and usefulness of the Pestalozzian system; indeed, to see Pestalozzi's method
displayed before his eyes and to form an unalter-
able wish of naturalizing it in his own country,
were operations succeeding each other with such
rapidity, that Mr. Maclure took them for one and
the same operation. As soon as he had returned
to Paris Mr. Maclure sought and sent for me.
'On what terms,' said the magnanimous patriot,
'would you go to my country and introduce there
your method of education? I have seen Pestalozzi; I know his system; my country wants it
and will receive it with enthusiasm. I engage to
pay your passage, to secure your livelihood. Go
and be your master's apostle in the new world.'
My soul was warmed with admiration at such uncommon generosity. Republican by inclination
and principle, and of course not at all pleased
with the new order of things that was established
under my eyes, I was not only glad to quit Europe,
but I burnt with desire to see that country, to
live in it, to be useful to it, which can boast of

such citizens. But what still heightens Mr. Maclure's magnanimity is that I did not at that period understand English at all. Two years at least were to be allowed for my acquiring a sufficient knowledge of the language of this land, during which space I had no other resource left me but Mr. Maclure's generosity. But neither this nor any other consideration could stagger his resolution."

The contract between Maclure and Neef, in the former's handwriting, was kindly loaned me by Neef's daughter, Mrs. Richard Owen. It is in a large round clear hand and reads: "Professor Neef agrees to go to Pennsylvania in the United States of America and to teach children after the methods of Pestalozzi for three years from the date of his arrival, in consequence of which Wm. Maclure agrees to pay Professor Neef's expenses from Paris to the U. S. of America to the amount of Three thousand two hundred Livres Tournois [about six hundred dollars] and to make good to Professor Neef whatever sum as salary he may receive for teaching said methods that falls short of Five Hundred Dollars per Annum during the three years or the time Professor Neef may continue to teach the system of Pestalozzi. Paris, 19th March, 1806 [signed] William Maclure." On the back of the same is the following: "Paris, 19th March, 1806. Received from Wm. Maclure Three Thousand two hundred Livres Tournois in full for my expenses to the U. S. of America agreeable to the terms of the Within Engagement [Signed] Neef." Here clearly was profound faith in the possibilities of Pestalozzianism! Well might Mr. Maclure's biographer say of him: "He devoted his talents and his wealth, not to the acquisition of a greater fortune or to personal aggrandizement or to sensual indulgence, but to the advancement of science and the amelioration of the condition of his fellow men, born and living in circumstances not as favorable to happiness as himself."

Mr. Neef devoted three years to the study of the English language and the educational needs of the new world. During this interval he wrote and published his *Sketch of a plan of education.* In 1809 he opened his school in Philadelphia which he continued successfully for more than three years when he removed the same to Village Green, in Delaware County, Pennsylvania. While here one David Glasgow Farragut, subsequently the famous American admiral, was a pupil. But the change proved disastrous, and after a little more than a year, upon the advice of Dr. Galt, a patron from Louisville, Kentucky, he removed his school thither. With the establishment of the social colony at New Harmony by Robert Owen in 1825, Neef joined the community in the capacity of schoolmaster. When the colony broke up in 1828 he removed to Cincinnati and later to Steubenville, Ohio, where he conducted schools during the next six years. He returned to New Harmony in 1834 where he continued to live up to the time of his death, April the 8th, 1854. His *Sketch of a plan and method of education,* as well as his educational labors in Philadelphia and at New Harmony, will be discussed in following chapters.

Those who knew Neef well describe him as being "a man of unusual abilities and eccentric character, a profound scholar, a deep and original thinker, a thorough philosopher and an honest man." In personal appearance he was "firm-knit, sinewy, compact of form with a bright, dark eye and close-cut coal black hair, the figure and gait of a well-drilled, graceful soldier, the face of a Roman Tribune, the mind of a sage, and the heart of a child." In spite of the fact that he is reported as having no inclinations for society, I find among the documents preserved by his daughter a certificate indicating membership in the Masonic lodge and election to membership in the Academy of Natural Sciences of Philadelphia.

One of the Philadelphia students[1] relates that "on occasions when it became necessary that he should visit the city, his wife, an excellent and notable woman, would tie a cravat (which he habitually went without) round his neck and put a hat on his head, much to his disgust and annoyance. 'Alas,' he would exclaim at such times with a mock resignation, 'must I again have that rope round my neck.' It usually happened, on these occasions citywards, that, taking off his hat in the stage, or at the first halt on his route, he forgot all about that superfluous article, and would return to his good lady hatless as usual. And if the day had been warm the cravat generally shared the fate of the hat. To guard against these frequently recurring losses, Mrs. Neef had recourse, finally, to the plan of attaching her husband's name and address to the inside of his headgear."

In the prospectus[3] of his Philadelphia school Mr. Neef tells prospective patrons with great frankness that he is little given to meaningless social conventionalities. He says: "To prevent my future visitors from all kinds of astonishment, I must apprise them before hand that they will probably find me rather refractory to the common laws of civility. I know very well that politeness is an indispensible duty of a sociable and social man; but I also know that there are duties of different descriptions. * * * To take care of my pupils will be my supreme duty, for which I will not hesitate to postpone even the laws of civility."

CHAPTER IV

Neef's Plan and Method of Education

Earliest American book on education. Connection with Pestalozzi. Aim of education. Function of oral instruction Method of object teaching. Use of books. Study of number and form. Grammar. Religious instruction. Physics. Gymnastics and physical training. Study of languages. Music and poetry. Geography. Sale of the book. Translation of Condillac's Logic. Neef's third book: Methods of teaching reading and writing.

Mr. Neef reached Philadelphia during the summer of 1806 but he devoted three years to a mastery of the English language and the preparation of his *Sketch of a plan and method of education*. Although Christopher Dock's *Schul-Ordnung* is the oldest American book on the art of teaching,* Neef's book may be said to be the first strictly pedagogical book written and published in the

*For an account of Christopher Dock and his *Schul-Ordnung*, see Samuel W. Pennypacker's *Historical and biographical sketches* (Philadelphia, 1883, pp. 91–153).

new world in the English language. The full title reads: *Sketch of a plan and method of education founded on the analysis of the human faculties and natural reason, fitted for the offspring of a free people and of all rational beings.* By Joseph Neef, formerly a co-adjutor of Pestalozzi at his school near Berne, Switzerland. Philadelphia; Printed for the author, 1808, pp. 168.

Recalling that the English language was a foreign tongue to Mr. Neef, the style of the book is singularly clear and forceful.

In the preface the author pays this tribute to his master: "There lives in Europe, beneath the foot of the Alps, an old man whose name is Pestalozzi, a man as respectable for the goodness of his heart as for the soundness of his head. This man, endowed by nature, or rather nature's god, with the felicity of an observing mind, was forcibly struck by the vices, follies, and extravagancies of the superior ranks, and the ignorance, superstition, and debasement of the inferior ranks of society. He perceived that from these impure sources flowed all the miseries that afflicted his unhappy fellow creatures. Being no disciple of Zeno, the woes of his brethern naturally imparted their anguish to his sensitive heart. The host of calamities, under which he saw his fellow men groaning, deeply grieved his feeling soul, and the gulf of evils, into which he viewed mankind plunged, called forth the most cordial and sincere compassion. Tears fell from his mourning eyes but they were manly tears. Far from being disheartened by such a sad spectacle, he had the courage to enquire into the causes of human misery; he went even a step farther and endeavored to find out a wholesome remedy, calculated to destroy at their very source those evils which inundate the world.

"Considering that man is born neither good nor bad, but that the disposition to become either good or bad is intimately interwoven with his organization, he became soon convinced that our education is the only cause of our becoming either good, useful, intelligent, rational, moral and virtuous beings, or wicked, noxious, ignorant, senseless, superstitious, and therefore miserable creatures. His mind was necessarily directed toward investigating the established systems of education; and after a mature examination thereof, he conceived that, without a radical reformation of the prevailing methods, it would be perfectly useless to expect any better results. This reformation became now the subject of his meditations. After having sufficiently digested these most important ideas, he began to communicate his thoughts to the world. In a plain but striking way he unfolded his plan of reformation and displayed the happy consequences to which it would lead. His book was read; his sagacity was admired; his benevolent counsels were applauded —and forgotten!* But he did not despond. The

*Pestalozzi's Leonard and Gertrude was published in 1781. It was widely praised. Madame de Staël declared it the most important book of the period, and the kings and queens of a dozen European countries decorated the author. Pestalozzi, however, was not seeking literary honors but an improved state of society.

same object was exposed to view over and over again, in all the forms and shapes of which it was susceptible; and yet was the desired reformation still to be begun and executed. Determined not to depart this life without at least seeing his theory tried, he resolved, in his old age, of making a full experiment of it himself. He therefore established a school. Other men, animated by his philanthropical enthusiasum, joined him; and thus began a work which will render Pestalozzi's name as dear and venerable to posterity as the deeds of many of his contemporaries will render them execrable to future generations."

Besides the introduction and conclusion, there are sixteen chapters in the *Sketch*, as follows: (1) Speech and speaking; (2) Number, arithmetic and calculation; (3) Geometry; (4) Drawing; (5) Writing and reading; (6) Grammar; (7) Ethics and morals; (8) Natural history; (9) Natural philosophy; (10) Chemistry; (11) Exercise and gymnastics; (12) The study of languages; (13)

Music; (14) Poetry; (15) Geography, and (16)
Lexicology.

In his introduction Neef defines education as
the gradual unfolding of the faculties and powers
which Providence bestows on the noblest work
of creation—man. Nature gives every human
being physical, intellectual and moral capacity.
The new born child contains the germs of these
faculties just as the acorn contains the germs of
the majestic oak; and the work of the teacher
is the unfolding of these powers—to train the
child to make just use of its faculties.

He denies that Pestalozzi's scheme is new and
affirms that there is nothing new under the sun.
Pupils will learn the same old arts and sciences
but they will learn them in a new way. "This
new way is Pestalozzi's method, which, as you
will perceive by and by, essentially and funda-
mentally differs from all other systems of education. Pestalozzi does not attempt to introduce
anything into his pupil, but to develop what he
finds in him. The first and fundamental point

being found out, he proceeds from thence neither by jumps, nor starts, nor giant strides. *Festina lenté* is a principle, a rule, which guides all his steps. His pupil always sets out from the known and plain, and proceeds with slow speediness to the yet unknown and complicated. He leaves no point behind him without being perfectly master of it. Every point of knowledge which he acquires is but a step to acquire a new one; all his faculties are displayed but none is overtrained; all his proceedings are subject to the minutest gradation."

Neef's method of approach throughout is essentially the same as that of his master. Violence is not done to the child by thrusting him into the intricacies of the printed page. Oral language is in consequence the starting point with the young learner. In order to cultivate and unfold the power of speaking, it is necessary to unfold all the powers of the mind. Neef regards the acquisition of language and the communication of ideas and thoughts by means of articulate sounds as the basis of all elementary school training. This means he would attain through the study of the natural objects in the child's environment. The eleven steps in such object instruction (oral language) are (1) study of the object as a whole; (2) determine the coherency, subordination, connection or relation between two objects, or between the part and whole of an object; (3) examine the number of things; (4) point out the position or situation of the object; (5) point out the qualities of the object; (6) form or shape of the object; (7) organic functions of the object; (8) uses we may make of the object; (9) resemblance of this object with other somewhat similar objects; (10) difference of this object with other objects studied; (11) summary—an exact and precise description of all that has been observed investigated, analyzed and determined in the preceding steps.

By means of a system of object teaching, children will not only acquire vocabularies, but will acquire skill in the expression of thought and capacity to form judgments. "All possible knowledge which in any way we shall be able to derive from our own senses and immediate sensations, shall be exclusively derived from them. The second source to which we shall next resort, but only in those cases where the first will be absolutely inaccessible shall be our memory; our third resource shall be analogy. Human evidence shall not be neglected, but we shall only have recourse to it when all the foregoing means prove insufficient and unsuccessful. *Books, therefore, shall be the last fountain from which we shall endeavor to draw our knowledge.*" Neef shared with Pestalozzi profound distrust for bookish knowledge.*

*In rejecting superficial book-learning as an empty mockery, Pestalozzi said: "A man who has only word wisdom is less susceptible to truth than a savage. This use of mere words produces men who believe they have reached the goal, because their whole life has been spent in talking about it, but who never ran toward it, because no motive impelled them to make the effort; hence, I come to the conviction that the fundamental error—the blind use of words in matters of instruction—must be extirpated before it is possible to resuscitate life and truth."

In the study of numbers, combinations must be made by means of objects and the child must acquire abstract notions of unity and plurality by means of objects that are studied. Every mathematical statement should be understood and a child should be encouraged to contradict any principle or rule which does not tally with his own understanding and experience. "My pupils shall never believe what I tell them, because I tell it to them; but because their own senses and understanding tell them that it is true. If your pupils ventured to tell you that you were wrong and mistaken, when you were really so, you would believe your magesterial dignity, authority and infallibility to be wounded and outraged; and, in order to avenge them, you would punish and chastise the little daring culprit and thus prevent his repeating the heinous crime. But I, on the contrary, shall require and exact of my pupils to tell me as loud as they can and as they please, that I am wrong, whenever their understanding tells them that I am really so."

Form study, it will be remembered, occupied an important place in Pestalozzi's scheme of elementary school instruction, and form study was an inductive approach to geometry. Here, as in arithmetic, the child must understand all that is taught him; and if he is to understand geometry, the study must be concretely and inductively developed. Neef did not think it wise to teach geometry from a book but rather to develop with the class, by means of models and drawings, the elements of geometry. He says: "Instead of teaching my pupils, instead of demonstrating to them the successively occurring theorems and problems, instead of crowding into their heads an infinity of half-understood, misunderstood, and very frequently not-at-all understood rules and precepts, I shall on the contrary, act the mere part of a disciple. The teacher's part will entirely devolve on them. My only task will be to present, in their successive order, the theorems to be demonstrated and the problems to be solved."

With reference to the study of grammar Neef

is explicit to state that he regards the foundations of all languages as grounded upon grammatical knowledge; but he does not regard the study of a text-book as essential to such grammatical knowledge.   Rather, he thinks, the grammar of a language should be deduced from the use of the language.   In a word: "My pupils shall compose their own grammar."

Mr. Neef was not a believer in dogmatic religious instruction in the schools.   If children were to be instructed in religious dogmas at all, he thought such instruction should be given in the home.   He believed thoroughly in moral and ethical instruction which "will acquaint children with their inalienable rights and immutable duties in a moral world;" and he thought the Golden Rule the safest basis for such instruction.

All school studies are to be regarded merely as the means by which the natural faculties of the mind shall be brought to their maturity; and of all school studies, natural history presents unquestionably the best and most convenient means

to effect that purpose. The interest of the child
is a cardinal principle in Neef's scheme of instruction* and he regards natural history as best calculated to awaken the interests of young children.
But the child is not to learn natural history from
books but from nature. He shall "observe, examine, analyze and describe all the various earths,
stones, salts, bitumens, metals, vegetables, trees,
plants, quadrupeds, birds, worms, insects and
fishes which we shall successively discover in our
constant excursions." The school garden is recommended as a most useful agent in the study of

*One hundred years ago Neef must have stood quite alone
in America in his advocacy of the doctrine of interest. Today
the doctrine is generally accepted by thoughtful school men.
Nicholas Murray Butler well says of the doctrine: "The proper
and scientific course is to search for the pupil's empirical and
natural interests, and to build upon them. This is not always
easy; it requires knowledge, patience and skill. It is far easier
to treat the entire class alike and to drive them over the hurdles
set by a single required course of study, in the vain hope that the
weak and the timid will not be injured as much as the strong
and confident will be benefited; and that somehow or other the
algebraic sum of the results of the process will bear a positive
sign."

natural history in familiarizing children with the manipulation and cultivation of plants. All such study should develop the humane instincts of the children, since "the citizens of the animal world are very near relations of ours."

Many of the laws of physics are simple and may be acquired by the child without premeditated design. The rising and setting of the sun, the different phases of the moon, the havoc of the thunder-storm, the changes from summer to winter, the pressure and equilibrium of bodies, the nature of liquids—these, and many other natural forces, may be taught and understood by observation. Similarly with the study of chemistry. The kitchen may serve as the laboratory and the food substances the subjects for an elementary study of chemistry.

One of the most valuable chapters of the book is that devoted to gymnastics and physical training. It will be recalled that he taught the gymnastics during his connection with Pestalozzi's school at Burgdorf and in succeeding chapters it will be noted that gymnastics received important consideration in the schools which he conducted at Philadelphia and New Harmony. "The most superficial observer of children," he points out, "must be forcibly struck with their untamable activity, with their great predilection for bodily exercises, with their untired fondness for running, jumping, climbing, bathing, and swimming, and that they always prefer the fresh open air, however cold or hot, to the inclosed air of a house."

He considers it just as wise to remove young and growing plants from all communication with air, light, and water as to prevent children from conforming to their unquestionable instincts and imperious wants. "My pupils shall run, jump, climb, slide, skate, bathe, swim and exert their adroitness, display their dexterity and exercise their bodily force, just as much as they please, or at least as it is rational to allow them."

If a child's bodily faculties are to be unfolded and improved, surely the school must provide the means of such unfoldment and improvement. He outlines a scheme of gymnastics and advocates definite military training; not that he believes in the principle of war—for he does not— but he thinks that every boy should have the training and hardihood to defend successfully his personal rights and liberties as well as the rights and liberties of his country.

In his discussion of the study of languages Neef is pronounced in his opposition to the ancient languages and he refutes with extraordinary vigor the arguments usually offered in defense of such study. First, as to utility, he maintains that in the countries of Europe very few scholars are able to speak the Latin and Greek. He denies that the classical authors furnish helpful models in composition. Correct thinking he maintains is never acquired from a foreign language—ancient or modern. One's thinking must always be done in one's mother tongue. Neither is it an argument for the study of the ancient languages to say that English contains so many Latin and

Greek words. The same argument might be made for the study of German, Keltic, French, Swedish, and a dozen other languages. When taught as an oral language, when the spoken language precedes the study of written language and when grammatical forms are not made the basis of the study, Neef believes that the study of a modern language—and preferably the French—may have distinct educational value.

Music is regarded as an essential study in the elementary school course and Neef offers an argument that I do not recall to have heard before —viz., that the study of vocal music improves materially the quality of the speaking voice. Literature in the form of poetry is considered of special value because of the element of rhythm.

In the study of geography, the school world is naturally the starting point, the pupils making their own maps. Home geography (Heimatskunde), it will be remembered, was one of the striking innovations of Pestalozzi; and all such instruction was given in the open air and in the presence of the geographic forms and forces being studied. Many of Neef's views strike one as singularly new to-day and many of the reforms which he advocated are still advocated by leaders of advanced educational thought.

By 1826 Maclure tells us the edition of the *Sketch* was completely exhausted and the book has never since been re-published; but that it warrants re-publication, thoughtful readers of this brief summary, I think, will grant. In addition to the *Sketch*, Neef published two other books. His second book was a translation of Condillac's *Logic*. The full title reads: *The logic of Condillac. Translated by Joseph Neef as an illustration of the plan of education established at his school near Philadelphia. Philadelphia, 1809. pp. 138.* It is a literal translation without notes or comments. His third book was: *The method of instructing children rationally in the arts of writing and reading. By Joseph Neef. Philadelphia, 1813. pp. 388.* This book is in reality an elaboration of his views of reading and writing outlined in his first book.

In the preface he writes: "Whether my plan be good or bad, better or worse than others, is to be decided by those who make proper trial of it; and to them I dedicate the following instructions for teachers." Ninety-five pages are devoted to a discussion of methods of teaching reading (and writing) and the balance of the book to exercises calculated to illustrate the method. Neef combined the phonetic and sentence methods in teaching reading, and writing was taught in connection with reading. It will be recalled that Neef postponed considerably the process of word-learning. Only after children had acquired large vocabularies of common objects and expressed themselves with freedom and clearness about these objects, would he introduce the mechanical phase of reading.* The *Method* is about the only reading

*Modern psychological scholarship is quite in accord with Mr. Neef in thus postponing the formal part of reading until a later period. Professor George Thomas White Patrick, in an able article, "Should children under ten be taught to read and write?" in the *Popular Science Monthly* for January 1899 (Vol. 54, pp. 382-392), argues that they should not. Says Professor

book to be used by children. When they mastered that he would give them good literature. Mr. Neef's daughter wrote me that her father also prepared a fourth book giving his methods of teaching the French language, but that the manuscript never was printed.

Patrick in this connection: "If the child at this age [between five and ten] must be put into the harness of an educational system, his course of study will not be impoverished by the omission of reading and writing. To teach him to speak and to listen, to observe and to remember, to know something of the world around him, and instinctively to do the right thing, will furnish more than enough material for the most ambitious elementary school curriculum."

CHAPTER V

FIRST AMERICAN PESTALOZZIAN SCHOOL AT PHILADELPHIA

School at the Falls of the Schuylkill. Buildings. Method of teaching arithmetic. Out-door life. Physical training and sports. Reminiscences of a pupil. Discipline. Military exercises. Removal of the school. School at Village Green: David Glasgow Farragut a pupil. Removal of the school to Louisville.

The employment of Joseph Neef by William Maclure for the organization of a Pestalozzian school in Philadelphia, and Neef's views on educational methods and principles, have been told in preceding chapters. Late in the summer of 1809 the first Pestalozzian school in America was opened in the suburbs of Philadelphia, at the Falls of the Schuylkill, near where the Fairmount Water Works are now located. "There were actual falls in those days," relates one of the original pupils [2] of the school, "the sounds of the rapids could be heard for a mile or more, and it was no uncommon sight to behold the Indian steering his canoe skillfully and calmly down through the whirling waters. But the Fairmount Water Works were subsequently built, a dam was constructed across the stream, and the water so far backed as to cover the rocks and obliterate the falls altogether."

The school house was situated on a hill and near it were two other buildings, used as the dwelling house and dormitories. They were plainly built, of rough, substantial material, but they were well ventilated and comfortable. On this spot, as Mr. Gardette[2] tells us, Mr. Neef succeeded in collecting over one hundred boys, most of them sons of the best families residing in and about Philadelphia and nearly all of them boarders. A kinsman of Mr. Gardette has thus described the institution: "I lived at the school for four years—from my seventh to my eleventh year. During this period I saw no book, neither was I taught my alphabet. The chief subjects—

languages, mathematics and the natural sciences —were taught us orally; and the idea was to make us understand the object and application of all we learned."

Neef's method of teaching mathematics is thus sketched: "Great blackboards hung in the school-rooms and the method of indoor instruction was as follows: Arithmetic, for instance being the matter in hand, and the rule of three (the highest point I ever reached there) the special problem, a pupil was chosen from the class who chalked upon the blackboard such a statement as 4:16::7:28, and having given the proof in the peculiar manner adopted by Neef and explained in his book, [4] he called the statement and demonstrated aloud, and the entire class repeated after him, over and over, till they were fully impressed on their minds. The power of memory—especially for numbers obtained by the pupils in this way, was remarkable. Little boys of ten or twelve would multiply by tens of thousands promptly, without slate or pencil, or give correct answers in the rule of three, no matter how great the figures, as quickly as you would have it worked out on paper."[2]

As all knowledge of common objects was obtained at first hand—no books being used—Neef spent much of the school time in the open air with his pupils studying home geography and natural history. The student already quoted relates in this connection: "Our outdoor life was equally curious. We never wore hats, winter or summer, and many of us went barefooted also during the warm weather. Our master, hatless as ourselves, would lead us on long tramps through the adjacent country, talking as we went, upon agriculture, botany, mineralogy and the like, in a pleasant descriptive way, and pointing out their practical illustration in the grain fields, the gardens, the rocks and streams along our route. And wherever we came we were always recognized by our bare heads and hardy habits as 'the Neef boys from the Falls.'"

Physical exercises of a natural but vigorous sort occupied a commanding place in Neef's

scheme of education. Says Mr. Gardette's kinsman: "We were encouraged in all athletic sports,
were great swimmers and skaters, walkers and
gymnasts. In the pleasant weather we went
to bathe twice every day in the Schuylkill, with
Neef, who was an accomplished swimmer, at our
head. It was probably owing to these amusements and exercises being taken in common with
our master that there existed between Neef and
his pupils so great a freedom as to be sometimes,
I fear, slightly inconsistent with good breeding or
the deference due from pupil to teacher. But
this seemed to be a part of the system, and Mr.
Neef was a thoroughly good natured, simple-
mannered, and amiable man, without an atom of
false pride or pedagogism."[2] How like the char-
acterization, quoted in a previous chapter, by
Ramsauer, who was a pupil in Pestalozzi's school
at Burgdorf while Neef still taught there.

Until the children had reached the age of ten or
eleven, Neef did not consider books suitable tools
for the education of youth, and he put his theory

into practice in the Philadelphia school. He wrote on this subject: "It is irrevocably decided and determined that my pupils shall pry into no book, turn over no book, read no book, till they are able not only to comprehend what they read, but also to distinguish perfectly well good from bad, truth from falsehood, reality from chimera, and probabilities from absurdities. God's beautious and prolific creation—all nature—shall be their book, and facts their instructors. But as soon as they shall have reached the necessary maturity, then, and only then, shall they read; then their reading will be really useful, and both instructive and pleasing to them." It was Neef's conviction the mechanical phases of reading and writing were begun altogether too early in the school-life, and it is a fact worth recording that the best modern psychological thought is in entire accord with Mr. Neef.

Neef was at all times on a footing with his pupils; he regarded himself as a fellow learner; the problem of discipline was in consequence solved, since his school was self-governing. On this point he writes:[4] "The grave, doctorial, magisterial, and dictatorial tone shall never insult their ears; they shall probably never hear of cat-o'-nine-tails. I shall be nothing else but their friend and guide, their school-fellow, play-fellow, and messmate."

In all essential particulars, the Pestalozzian school at Philadelphia differed from contemporaneous American institutions. Gardette tells us that instead of ringing a bell, Neef always called the boys together by whistling three times in a peculiar way. He did this by placing his crooked forefinger between his teeth and uttering a prolonged note, loud and shrill enough to be heard a long way off.

A military man himself, Mr. Neef believed implicitly in the educational value of military training, and it is to be feared that he not only permitted but encouraged certain vigorous and questionable forms of physical exercise, such as wrestling and fighting.*   This met with no small amount of condemnation on the part of those patrons of the school who were members of the Society of Friends.   In reply to such criticism he said that he had no hand in the making of society what it is and he doubted if it was likely to be much better in the days of his grandchildren; but he maintained that in such a state of society as the present, it was necessary for every lad to acquire the courage and the physical skill to defend his "life and liberty against any invader, human, in-human or super-human in shape."   He argued that military drills appealed to the interests of boys and related an experience during his con-nection with Pestalozzi's school at Burgdorf

*G. Stanley Hall in his new work on *Adolescence* remarks in this connection: "Better even an occasional nose dented by a fist, a broken bone, a rapier-scarred face, or even the sacrifice of an occasional life of our best academic youth than stagnation, general cynicism and censoriousness, bodily and psychic coward-ice, and moral corruption, if this indeed be, as it sometimes is, its real alternative."

where much good was accomplished for the boys by such drills. [4]

The Philadelphia school was altogether prosperous and the only reason for its removal that I have ever been able to learn was the desire of Mr. Neef to locate in the country and thus give his pupils the full advantages of out-door life and the study of nature. Before the fourth year had ended he removed his school to Village Green in Delaware County, near the city of Chester. A large number of the pupils in the Philadelphia school accompanied him; and Phiquepal d' Arusmont, an eccentric Frenchman, who was later connected with Neef in the educational work of the New Harmony community, accompanied him to Village Green as assistant teacher.

The only noteworthy fact to be recorded in the history of the Village Green experience was the membership in the school of a lad who subsequently became a distinguished admiral in the navy of the United States—David Glasgow Farragut. Young Farragut's father had died and

Captain (afterwards Admiral) Porter had taken charge of the lad. He went with Porter on the ill-fated cruise of the Essex which was captured by the British in the war of 1812. In common with the other survivors of the Essex, Farragut landed in New York as a paroled prisoner of war.

Porter took him at once to Chester and placed him in Neef's school. Writing in his later life Admiral Farragut gives this account of his experiences at Neef's school: "I accompanied my friend Captain Porter to Chester, where I was put in a school to a queer old individual named Neef. His method of instruction was simple in the extreme; he had no books but taught orally such subjects as he desired us to understand. The scholars took notes and were afterwards examined on these lectures. In the afternoon it was customary for us to take long walks, accompanied by our instructor. On these occasions Mr. Neef would make collections of minerals and plants, and talk to us about mineralogy and botany. The course of study was not very regular but we certainly had an opportunity of gaining a great deal of useful information and worldly knowledge. We were taught to swim and climb, and were drilled like soldiers—branches of instruction to be accounted for, probably, by the fact that the old gentleman had been one of Napoleon's celebrated guards. I do not regret the time passed at this school, for it has been of service to me all my life." [1]

The removal to Village Green turned out to have been unwise and the number of students rapidly declined. Neef himself held rather broad views on religious matters and he was accused by his rural neighbors of inculcating atheistic ideas in the minds of his boys. This charge was absolutely groundless, but the school suffered nevertheless from the criticisms. Neef grew discouraged; and when, in 1816, Dr. Galt of Louisville, Kentucky, two of whose sons were in the school, visited Village Green, and urged him to remove his school to Louisville, Neef unwisely acted upon the suggestion. Few of his old students cared to accompany him at so great a distance, and Louisville at that time was a town of little more than five thousand inhabitants. The school did not prosper as Dr. Galt had hoped it would; and after a couple years of effort, Neef grew discouraged, abandoned teaching, and purchased a farm in the country, about twenty-five miles from Louisville. Here he continued to reside until his call to New Harmony in 1825.

CHAPTER VI

In the chapter on William Maclure and the earliest introduction of Pestalozzian ideas in the United States, some of the facts concerning the educational activities of the New Harmony community have already been pointed out. While the community was in the main an ex-

*The New Harmony Community was an experiment in co-operative socialism. The purpose is stated by Robert Owen, its founder, was: (1) the introduction of changes in the social and industrial structure of society necessitated by the increased productive power of the age; (2) the establishment of co-operative industry which should replace competitive labor; and (3) the organization of society into communities of 1500 or 2000 people

pression of the social ideals of Robert Owen, the educational interests were entrusted to William Maclure; and Mr. Maclure called Joseph Neef and other Americanized Pestalozzians to his assistance in working out his educational experiment.

In his *Epitome of the improved Pestalozzian system* Mr. Maclure says: "The great and fundamental principle is never to attempt to teach children what they cannot comprehend, and to teach them in the exact ratio of their understanding it, without omitting one link in the chain of ratiocination, proceeding always from the known to the unknown, from the most easy to the most difficult, practicing the most extensive and accurate use of all the senses, exercising, improving and perfecting all the mental and corporeal fac-

who should own land and houses in common and labor for the benefit of the community. Mr. Owen wished to avoid the evils of large cities and the disadvantages of solitary homes and to enable labor saving power to aid and not to oppress the workmen. For an account of the experiment at New Harmony see the works by Hill, Lockwood, Maclure, Robert Owen, Robert Dale Owen, and Packard given in section VI of the bibliography at the end of this volume.

ulties by quickening combination, accelerating and carefully arranging comparison, judiciously and impartially making deduction, summing up the results free from prejudices and cautiously avoiding the delusions of imagination, the constant source of ignorance and error." This was Mr. Maclure's conception of the function of the school.

The New Harmony community was organized in 1825, when Mr. Neef was called from Louisville to take immediate charge of the school. The official organ of the society, the New Harmony *Gazette*, had declared: "The society regards education as public property and holds that the educating and training of youth should be among the first objects of its solicitude and care." The work of teaching during the two brief years of the community's existence seems to have been shared by a number of persons—William Maclure, Joseph Neef, Thomas Say, Phiquepal d'Arusmont, Madame Neef, Madame Frotegeot, and others,—but

Neef, the co-adjutor of Pestalozzi, seems to have served as head master, and Mr. Maclure as superintendent of education.

Boys and girls were given the same kind of education in separate school-rooms, since the New Harmony community held to the theory of sex equality. In addition to the boarding schools for boys and girls, there was an infant school, modelled after the one Robert Owen had established at New Lanark, Scotland, for the training of children below the accepted school age. It was provided that children should become the property of the community at the age of two years, when they were first received into the infant school. This was essentially a play school; games were taught the children; playthings were provided, and "they were taught nothing they could not understand." The infant school was in charge of Madame Neef and Madame Frotegeot, who had conducted a Pestalozzian school in Philadelphia before coming to New Harmony.

William C. Woodbridge[8] visited the New

Harmony community shortly after its organization in 1825 and wrote: "There are four hundred children belonging to the society, besides those of strangers from various parts of the Union. The number, when all are organized, will be sufficient to occupy three large buildings. Of these, one will be that known among the Harmonians by the name of the Steeple House. Its dimensions are sixty feet by forty, height two stories. The upper part will serve for upwards of a hundred boys to sleep, the lower part is divided into workshops for shoemakers, tailors, carpenters, tinmen, stocking weavers, etc., at which the boys all learn to work part of their time as a recreation from more studious pursuits, besides being occasionally employed in the fields and gardens, all of which are cultivated on the most improved principles of agriculture adopted in any part of the world. All these exercises are substituted for the gymnastics of the old schools, and are equally strengthening for the body and may be made the means of training them to activity and energy so useful in the common occupations of life. The boys already can make their own shoes, clothes, etc., and in a short time may be able to furnish those articles to the whole community.

"At the same time they learn intellectual arithmetic, geography, mathematics, etc., for trades are used instead of play, and as an amusement when the boys are tired of mental work. One hundred and fifty girls of all ages, under the direction of Madame F., are taught the same as the boys, that is, drawing, music, arithmetic, mathematics, natural philosophy, a little chemistry, etc., The older girls are divided into classes. One class takes by turns the cooking, another the washing, a third keeping the house in order, a fourth the manufacture of cotton wool, for there are no servants in the society: all work, never working long at the same time, no class occupied above half of a day and at the same work, which makes it easy, and not fatiguing. Children have hitherto been unjustly treated; their time made a burthen to them, for want of occupation agreeable to their inclinations and faculties; for when properly managed, instead of being a burthen, they might be made a help to all connected with them. Experimental farming schools is one of the plans long had in view, where children would not only be well educated, but turn the help-part of their education into the means of feeding and clothing them. From the talents of the instructors, and the superiority of the machinery, this place will probably be the first in the union for a useful education."

William Russell published in the *American Journal of Education* for June 1826 extracts from a letter written to him from New Harmony under date of March the 31st, 1826, which states that "upwards of a hundred packages of books, etc., have just arrived via New Orleans. The works are the most useful and the most splendid that could be procured on natural history, antiquities, architecture, agriculture, etc. There is besides an extensive collection of paintings and prints. Our teachers are Messrs. Neef, Phiquepal, T. Say,

and several other eminent foreigners. We do
not hesitate to say that this place offers advantages for education which are not surpassed, if
equalled, by any part of this country. The expenses
attending the education, board, etc., of one pupil
are not over one hundred dollars per annum; and,
when we get everything properly organized, will
not exceed half that sum." In commenting on
the letter Mr. Russell remarks: "The munificent
provisions for education in New Harmony, are
derived, we are told, from the liberality of an individual [William Maclure] who is extensively
known for his generous patronage of education
in various parts of the United States, and to whom
the monitorial school of this city [Boston] is indebted for a valuable cabinet of minerals."

The library movement, since become such a
prominent feature of educational work, was
prominent at New Harmony. When Owen
reached New Harmony from England in the mid-
dle of January 1826, he brought with him, besides
his son Robert Dale Owen, Thomas Say, Charles

Lesueur, and Gerard Troost, "a ship load of books." Lecture halls, reading rooms, and museums of natural history and mineralogy were also features of the work; for both Owen and Maclure were ardent advocates of what we call to-day university extension; and they were solicitous for the intellectual improvement of the adult members of the community as well as of the children.

The Duke of Saxe-Weimar visited the community schools in April 1826 and writes: "I found Professor Neef in the act of leading the boys of his school out to labor. Military exercise formed a part of the exercise of the children. I saw the boys divided into two ranks and parted into detachments, marching to labor. On the way they performed various wheelings and evolutions. All the boys and girls have a healthy look, are cheerful and lively, and by no means bashful. The boys labor in the fields and gardens; the girls learn house-hold employments; these happy and interesting little children are employed in making their youth pass as happily as possible."

The Duke also visited the dormitories where they were exercised in various forms of manual labor. The forms of manual training taught in the schools were carpentery, shoemaking, lithography and engraving.

Robert Dale Owen,[5] in his autobiographical sketches, gives this picture of the headmaster of the New Harmony schools: "Simple, straight-forward and cordial, a proficient in modern languages, a good musician, he had brought with him from Pestalozzi's institution an excellent mode of teaching. To his earlier life, as an officer under Napoleon, was due a blunt, off-hand manner and an abrupt style of speech, enforced now and then with an oath—an awkward habit for a teacher, which I think he tried ineffectually to get rid of. One day when I was within hearing, a boy in his class used profane language. 'Youngster,' said Neef to him, 'You mustn't swear. It's silly and it's vulgar and it means nothing. Don't let me hear you do so again.'

" 'But, Mr. Neef,' said the boy, 'if, if it's vulgar and wrong to swear, why ——'

" 'Well, out with it. Never stop when you want to say anything; that's another bad habit. You wished to know why ——'

" 'Why do you swear yourself, Mr. Neef?'

" 'Because I am a damned fool. Don't you be one too.' "

"With all his roughness," adds Mr. Owen, "the good old man was a general favorite, alike with children and adults. Those whose recollections of Harmony extend back to the forties preserve a genial remembrance of him, walking about in the sun of July or August, in linen trousers and shirt, always bareheaded, with a grandchild in his arms, and humming to his infant charge some martial air in a wonderful bass voice, which, it is said, enabled him in his younger days, when giving command to a body of troops, to be distinctly heard by ten thousand men."

Differing on many questions concerning the administration of the community, on one question both Maclure and Owen were agreed—viz., that no dogmatic sectarian religious instruction should be given in the schools. Mr. William C. Woodbridge, writing again in the *American Journal of Education* (Boston) for March 1827, says: "The system [at New Harmony] is the improved Pestalozzian; and of course they never attempt to teach children what they cannot comprehend. In consequence, all kinds of dogmas of every sect and persuasion are banished from the schools, but the purest and unsophisticated morals are taught by example and precept. In the infant school a friendly feeling and equanimity of temper, kindness, and mild disposition toward one another is taught more by example than by precept."

Much time was spent out of doors in the study of natural history and the collection of objects for study in the school-rooms. Sir Rowland Hill, an Englishman, who visited New Harmony commends this system of natural education and remarks that the children "swarm over the woods and bring in such an abundance of specimens that they are forming several immense collections, some of which they will present to new communities, and others will be exchanged for collections in other parts of the world."

Mrs. Sarah Cox Thrall, who was a pupil in the girls' department of the community schools at New Harmony, has left some reminiscences of her own experiences. The girls, she says, wore dresses of coarse linen in summer for ordinary wear, with coarse plaids for Sunday and special occasions. In winter they wore dresses of wool. At rising the girls did the morning milking of the cows. The morning meal consisted of mush and milk. After breakfast they marched to school to military orders. "I remember," she writes, "that there were blackboards covering one side of the schoolroom, and that we had wires with balls on them by which we learned to count. We also had singing exercises by which we familiarized ourselves with lessons in various branches. At dinner we generally had soup, at supper mush and milk again. We went to bed at sun-down in little bunks suspended in rows by cords from the ceiling." She mentions that the children were permitted to see their parents only at rare intervals. [2]

Maclure and Owen differed rather widely in their opinions of educational practice. Mr. Owen desired great uniformity in subjects and methods, whereas Mr. Maclure advocated unbounded freedom. Mr. Owen desired more of the mechanism of the Lancastrian system but Maclure opposed the laying down of precise rules. In his autobiography Mr. Owen was inclined to blame the schools in part for the failure of the New Harmony experiment [4]; but this blame was clearly misplaced. The community was in existence less than two years and during this brief period the wholesale regeneration of society by the schools was not possible. New Harmony was visited by many eminent American and European educators and all spoke of the schools in terms of praise, one authority declaring that "the New Harmony system of education is the best in the world."

It must be admitted, however, that neither the Philadelphia school nor the New Harmony experiment influenced widely and permanently American education. The late Norman A. Calkins thought the cause of Neef's failure to markedly influence the educational practices of the new world, was due to the fact that he "failed to comprehend the necessity of Americanizing the Pestalozzian system instead of merely transplanting it." A somewhat careful study of Neef's published writings on education and of the character of his teaching in America does not sustain Mr. Calkins's point. Three other and different reasons explain Neef's failure to introduce permanently the educational doctrines of his master in the United States. First, the educational labors of Neef lacked permanency. He was in Philadelphia, it is true, more than seven years, but his school there was in actual operation less than four years. He was at Chester only two years. Had he remained in and about Philadelphia where his labors met with a measure of success and where his ideas were appreciated and endorsed, his name to-day might be one of the best known in the annals of the history of American education. But removal to the wilds of Kentucky crippled permanently the extension of Pestalozzian doctrines in the United States. Secondly, he devoted his time to the education of boys who later engaged in professional and industrial callings. Had his efforts been more directly concerned with the training of teachers, he might have trained disciples who would have spread the new educational gospel. This was contemplated as is apparent from the prospectus of his Philadelphia school published in 1808. "If any young men, who feel a disposition and inclination to to become teachers themselves and to become my associates and collaborators, they shall be welcome, and received as friends. All that I require of them is that they shall not be system-mongers; for this quality will render them unfit to learn the difficult art of forgetting their learning, and of descending from their lofty standing of mental acquirements to the low intellectual sphere of childhood." Thirdly, Neef came to America a quarter of a century too early. At the time of his arrival there were few generous souls like William Maclure profoundly interested in educational improvement. The renaissance of American education had not yet begun. Twenty-five years later the intellectual revival which developed educational leaders like William C. Woodbridge, Henry Barnard, Horace Mann, Walter Johnson, Thomas Gallaudet, Lowell Mason, Emma Willard, and a score of others, would have given Joseph Neef foremost rank in the great movement which organized our common school systems. In consequence of these facts, Mr. Neef's influence as an educator was less profoundly felt than was merited by the splendid experience and the towering intellectual strength of the man; and his labors in our country are forgotten or remembered only by a few special students of the history of education. The closing paragraph of the *Sketch of a plan and method of education* was, indeed, sadly prophetic of his subsequent career: "Should my project of forming my own school miscarry, then the director of some already established seminary will perhaps please to accept my service; and if this should not be the case, I shall in all likelihood find out some remote, obscure village whose hardy youth want a schoolmaster. Hear it, ye men of the world! To become an obscure, useful country schoolmaster is the highest pitch of my worldly ambition."

CHAPTER VII

PESTALOZZIANISM IN NEW ENGLAND

Earliest New England advocates. The private normal schools. William Russell: His educational labors. Normal school at Lancaster. James G. Carter: Efforts to improve public schools. Aids the establishment of normal schools. Charles Brooks: Missionary labors in behalf of normal schools. State normal schools in Massachusetts: Mr. Boutwell's claim of priority. The Westfield normal school and objective methods. William C. Woodbridge. His visit to Pestalozzi. Articles on Pestalozzian methods. Interest in vocal music. Bronson Alcott: Pestalozzian school at Cheshire. Mr. Alcott's methods. Labors in Boston and Philadelphia. The Temple school. Correspondence with Greaves. Lowell Mason: Pestalozzian methods in music. Experiments with children. Introduction of vocal music into the schools of Boston. State institutes and normal schools. Henry Barnard: Basis of early Pestalozzian interest. Visit to Fellenberg. Numerous Pestalozzian translations.

Pestalozzianism entered New England less early, and it influenced this section less markedly, than other parts of the United States. There were, nevertheless, from a relatively early period enthusiastic disciples of the Swiss reformer, particularly in Massachusetts and Connecticut. Among such New England disciples may be named William C. Woodbridge, A. Bronson Alcott, Lowell Mason, and Henry Barnard. Horace Mann was an ardent admirer of Pestalozzian institutions, as he saw them in Europe; and both Louis Agassiz and Arnold Guyot brought to New England from Switzerland the Pestalozzian spirit, and they employed the Pestalozzian method in their study and teaching of natural history and geography.

1   *William Russell*

The normal schools, both private and public, and the state teachers' institutes were early influenced by the doctrines of Pestalozzi. Among those who represented Pestalozzianism in the early private normal schools, mention should be made of the labors of William Russell, James G. Carter and Charles Brooks. William Russell

(1798-1873), who was born and educated in Scotland, came to the United States in 1817 to accept a position in an academy at Savannah, Georgia. After a few years in the south, he came north, teaching first in the Hopkins Grammar School in New Haven and later at the Theological Seminary at Andover and at Harvard College. He taught at Andover and Cambridge simultaneously the subjects of elocution and oratory. Deeply interested himself in the science of education, he began in 1826 the publication of a high grade review, the *American Journal of Education* (1826-1830). To except the *Academician* (1818-1819), which had an existence of a few months only, Russell's review was the first noteworthy attempt at educational journalism in the United States. It was published monthly in numbers of sixty-four octavo pages and five volumes were issued. William B. Fowle, Samuel R. Hall, Thomas H. Gallaudet, William C. Woodbridge, Wilbur Fisk, James G. Carter, A. Bronson Alcott, and Josiah Holbrook were among the American contributors;

and foreign educators were represented by translations and reprints from Pestalozzi, Jacotot,
Maria Edgworth, Jean Paul Richter, J. P. Greaves,
George Combe, and Elizabeth Harrison. Nine of
Pestalozzi's letters to Greaves were published
and a series of letters from Hofwyl, giving accounts
of Fellenberg's institution, written by William C.
Woodbridge. Mr. Russell was keenly interested
in the higher education of women, and in 1829 he
was called to Philadelphia to organize such an
institution. Upon his return to Boston he re-
sumed his former line of teaching at Andover and
at the same time engaged extensively in the work
of teachers' institutes in Massachusetts, under
Horace Mann, and in Rhode Island, under Henry
Barnard.

In 1849 he opened a private normal school in
New Hampshire. This was later removed to
Lancaster, Massachusetts. Its basis was dis-
tinctly Pestalozzian. William J. Whittaker and
Herman Krüsi, Jr., were brought from a Pestaloz-
zian school in England; and Dana P. Colburn and

Sanborn Tenney, both of whom had adopted the Pestalozzian method of instruction—the former in arithmetic and the latter in natural history—formed the remainder of the teaching staff. But the establishment and success of state normal schools in Massachusetts superseded the necessity of private establishments for the training of teachers; and Mr. Russell closed his institution at Lancaster in 1857 and devoted his closing years to lecture and literary work.

2 *James G. Carter*

"To James G. Carter (1795-1849), more than to any other person," says Henry Barnard, "belongs the credit of having first arrested the attention of the leading minds of Massachusetts to the necessity of immediate and thorough improvement in the system of free or public schools and of having clearly pointed out the most direct and thorough mode of procuring this improvement by providing for the competent training of teachers for these schools." Following his graduation from Harvard

College, Mr. Carter taught for several terms in the common schools, after which he established a private school at Lancaster. While here he began the agitation of common school reform, which culminated fifteen years later in the appointment of Horace Mann as secretary of the state board of education in Massachusetts.

In 1827 Mr. Carter presented to the legislature of Massachusetts a bill providing for the establishment of a normal school for the training of teachers, with a model or practice school attached. The memorial was favorably reported on by a committee in the house, of which the Hon. William B. Calhoun of Springfield was chairman, making an appropriation for the establishment of the same; but the bill was lost by one vote in the senate. He next endeavored to interest the town of Lancaster in the establishment of a private normal school; but his townsmen did not share his philanthropic sentiments and the movement failed. He continued to receive a number of young men in his own private school whom he trained for the work of teaching. He had become familiar with the plans and methods followed by Pestalozzi at Yverdon and he endeavored to apply the same in a small way at Lancaster. He was the moving spirit in the organization of the American Institute of Instruction in 1830, the oldest existing educational society in America, and he was a prominent speaker at many of its early meetings.

He was elected a member of the legislature in 1835, serving three years in the house of representatives and two years in the senate. He drafted the bill which established the Massachusetts state board of education and his vigor and intelligence were chief factors in its successful passage. Many of the best friends of education in Massachusetts were greatly disappointed that Mr. Carter was not selected as secretary of the board; but the subsequent splendid career of Horace Mann entirely justified the wisdom of the appointment of the board.

3   *Charles Brooks*

Charles Brooks (1795-1872) had visited Europe in the early thirties and had been deeply impressed with the efficient method of training teachers in the Pestalozzian normal schools in Germany. Accordingly, upon his return to Massachusetts, he instituted a series of public meeting for the agitation of the subject of a normal school in the old commonwealth. He organized and conducted such meetings in most of the towns of the state; and his powerful address before the legislature, making the first appropriation in behalf of normal schools, is one of the notable utterances in the history of the normal school movement. Mr. Barnard says in this connection, "Although not directly connected with the history of normal schools in Massachusetts, it may be mentioned in this place that no individual in the whole country has done more to arouse the public mind of New England to the importance of normal schools, and to some extent the leading minds of some other states, than the Rev. Charles Brooks." He was repeatedly called upon by the friends of education to plead their cause before the legislatures of New Hampshire, Vermont, Rhode Island, and Connecticut, as well as Massachusetts. In his ardent advocacy of the cause of normal schools in Massachusetts, one of the Boston newspapers represented him as "Captain Brooks, with ferrule in hand, at the head of a troop of schoolmasters and school mistresses, marching for a normal school in the clouds."

4   *Massachusetts Normal Schools*

The state normal schools of Massachusetts played also a part in promulgating the Pestalozzian doctrines, although they never became leaders in this movement to the extent of the normal school at Oswego, at a later date. The oldest normal schools in the United States, it will be recalled, are in Massachusetts. The Framingham and Westfield normal schools—the former at Lexington and the latter at Barre—were opened in 1839, the Bridgewater normal school in 1840 and the Salem normal school in 1853.

Mr George Sewell Boutwell (1818-1905), who was secretary of the state board of education of Massachusetts from 1853 to 1858, and who during that time advocated heartily the methods and doctrines of Pestalozzi, in a recent issue of the *Popular Science Monthly* takes issue with Mr. Aber that Oswego is entitled to the credit of introducing and promulgating over the country the system of teaching known as the Pestalozzian system. He says that, prior to 1860 [when the Oswego movement started], in at least four Massachusetts normal schools [Framingham, Westfield, Bridgewater and Salem], "the art of teaching was taught according to the system of Pestalozzi and by well informed teachers and professors, and with the knowledge that it was the system of Pestalozzi;" and that "previous to 1859 the art of teaching according to the system of Pestalozzi had been taught and the practice of the art had been illustrated to thousands of students in the normal schools and to teachers in the teachers' institutes in the state of Massachusetts."

5 *Westfield Normal School*

In his history of the Oswego movement, Mr. Hollis calls attention to the fact that the Westfield normal school was the pioneer in introducing object teaching into the schools; but he adds, "Unfortunately this valuable phase of the work at Westfield attracted little general attention; and it remained for another normal school in another state at a considerably later date, to demonstrate on an important scale the great value of object teaching in common school branches"

The Westfield normal school, as has been observed, was opened at Barre, September the third, 1839 with Samuel Phillips Newman (1797-1842) as principal. It was removed to Westfield in 1844 and Emerson Davis (1798-1866) served two years as principal. He was succeeded by David S. Rowe (1814-1888) who was principal of the school for eight years. William Henry Wells (1812-1885) succeeded Rowe in 1854; and upon Mr. Wells's election to the superintendency of the schools of Chicago two years later, John Woodbridge Dickinson (1825-1901) was chosen his successor. While object teaching had been a feature of the Westfield normal school from the time of its establishment, Mr. Dickinson is authority for the statement that after 1852 all the subjects in the school were taught by the analytic objective method. "These changes in the methods of teaching," he writes, "required a preparation of the means, so that there might be no violation of the principles upon which the method was founded. This turned the attention of the school to collecting such objects, illustrative apparatus, and reference books, as were necessary for a thorough system of objective teaching and study. The branches of learning required to be taught in the public schools were taken up, with special reference to teaching them to others in accordance with the laws of the human mind that control it in the acquisition of knowledge and devleopment of its faculties. That the pupils of the normal school might have an opportunity of observing the application of their methods to real children,

the town generously provided the school of observation, where they could add experience to
their theories. The results of these things soon
appeared in the professional spirit excited in the
different departments of the normal school, in the
improved work of its graduates, and in the new
interest which their good example produced
throughout the country in the study of the philosophy of education. The Westfield normal
school was the first to show that all branches of
learning may be taught by the same objective
method, and that elementary knowledge should
be taught with special and constant reference to
the scientific knowledge which is to be occasioned
by it." But the work at Westfield, as Mr. Hollis
remarks, did not attract widespread attention;
and, while it is true, as Mr. Boutwell contends,
that Massachusetts at an early date recognized
and practiced the methods of Pestalozzi, it is also
true that Massachusetts did not become a center
from which Pestalozzian influences radiated, as at
Oswego some years later.

6 *William C. Woodbridge*

As before suggested, however, the New England Pestalozzian movement found its chief supporters in William C. Woodbridge, A. Bronson Alcott, Henry Barnard and Lowell Mason. William Channing Woodbridge (1794-1845), following his graduation at Yale College in 1811, taught first in an academy at Burlington, New Jersey, and later in the deaf school at Hartford; but, feeling that he needed more light on educational problems, he went to Europe in 1820 and spent a year in study and travel. He was deeply impressed with the work and doctrines of Pestalozzi at Yverdon, and was much pleased with the agricultural phases of Fellenberg's institution at Hofwyl. He returned to America with marked enthusiasm for the introduction of the study of music in the common schools and with a quantity of material on the subject of geography. During the next three years he prepared and published his *Rudiments of geography* and his *Universal geography*. Dr. William A. Alcott writes in this connection:

W. B. Woodbridge

"Up to this period, geography as a science had received but little attention in the public schools of New England; with the exception of a few more favored of the larger schools, spelling, reading and writing were nearly all the branches that received special attention. A little arithmetic was taught here and there, but even this was for the most part crowded into the evening. * * * As for geography, some few schools studied Morse, a few others used a sort of reading book, Nathaniel Dwight's *System of geography*, which was arranged in the form of questions and answers. The vast majority, however, paid no attention to the subject. But Mr. Woodbridge, while instructing the deaf mutes at Hartford, and perhaps yet earlier, had hit upon an improved plan of teaching, which is now too well known, as incorporated into most of our school geographies, to need description. A similar method had been pursued by Mrs. Emma Willard (1787-1870) of the Troy Female Seminary. Both these teachers were preparing their plans of teaching for publication, unknown to each other; but Mrs. Willard was at length induced to merge her own work in that of Mr. Woodbridge. The Woodbridge and Willard geographies produced a revolution in the method of teaching this useful science."

Mr. Woodbridge returned to Europe again in 1825, spending three months with Pestalozzi and Fellenberg and visiting many Pestalozzian schools in Germany. He remained in Europe four years, visiting numerous institutions and collecting data on the general state of European education. Upon his return in 1829 he participated in the movement of the Society for the Improvement of the Common Schools which had been organized in Connecticut, whose purposes were the improvement of the common school, organization of institutions for the training of teachers, and improved facilities for the education of women. In 1831 he purchased from William Russell (1798-1873) the *American Journal of Education* which had been started in 1826.

The name was changed to the *American Annals of Education* and Mr. Woodbridge continued to edit the same until 1837, and at great pecuniary loss. It was high grade educational review, octavo in form, and each monthly number contained about forty-eight pages. Dr. William A. Alcott (1798-1859) was the associate editor and the seven volumes contain numerous articles on the Pestalozzian system of education. He returned to Europe again in 1836 but failing health prevented him from making the educational researches he had designed. He returned to America in 1841 but not improved in health and passed the next three winters at Santa Cruz. He died at Boston in November 1845. His biographer says of him: 'He was as influential as any man in awakening, and maintaining that interest in the cause of education generally which arose in Massachusetts between the years 1830 and 1840. He was an efficient agent in drawing public attention to the necessity of normal schools. He was, if not the very first, one of the earliest writers in favor of the introduction of the studies of physiology and vocal music into our schools. He drew from behind the counter of a country store, and introduced into the higher sphere, in which he has done so great and useful a work, the celebrated Lowell Mason, a service which alone would have made him a public benefactor." Mr. Woodbridge's letters in his own journal on Fellenberg's institution were among the first to appear in America; and he may be justly regarded as the pioneer in the movement which ultimately led to the introduction of vocal music into the schools of the United States.

At the first meeting of the American Institute of Instruction held at Boston in August 1830 Mr. Woodbridge gave an able and exhaustive paper on the Pestalozzian method in music. He noted that "the inductive system of instruction was introduced in Switzerland and Germany at the end of the last century by Pestalozzi, and had been adopted in this country in reference to some subjects. Early in the present century it was applied to music in the institution and under the direction of Pestalozzi by Pfeiffer and Nägeli, who published a manual of instruction on these principles in 1810. The system has since been diffused throughout the central portion of Europe, under various forms, and is now acknowledged, in its fundamental principles, to be the only true one." The principles of the Pestalozzian system of music, as there outlined by Mr. Woodbridge, are (1) To teach sounds before signs and to make the child learn to sing before he learns the written notes or their names; (2) to lead him to observe by hearing and imitating sounds, their resemblances and differences, their agreeable and disagreeable effect, instead of explaining these things to him— in a word, to make him active, instead of passive, in learning; (3) to teach but one thing at a time— rhythm, melody and expression to be taught and practiced separately, before the child is called to the difficult task of attending to all at once; (4) in making him practice each step of each of these divisions, until he is master of it, before passing to the next; (5) in giving the principles and theory after the practice, and as an induction from it; (6) in analyzing and practicing the elements of articulate sound in order to apply them to music; and (7) in having the names of the notes correspond to those used in instrumental music. According to Mr. Woodbridge, the Pestalozzian system of music instruction was first given practical trial by Mr. Ives in the schools of Hartford in 1830. Somewhat later, as will be seen in succeeding paragraphs, Lowell Mason became the American apostle of Pestalozzianism in music.

7   A. Bronson Alcott

Amos Bronson Alcott (1799-1888) was a Pestalozzian without knowing the basis of his pedagogic creed. To except Greaves's translation of Pestalozzi's *Letters on the early education of the child*, which fell into his hands shortly after the appearance of this work in Boston in 1830, and various stray articles on Pestalozzianism which

A. Bronson Alcott

appeared in the *American Journal of Education*
(1826-1831) and the *American Annals of Education* (1831-1837), to both of which journals Mr.
Alcott contributed occasional articles, evidence
is wanting to show that Mr. Alcott possessed in-
timate knowledge of the exact nature of Pestalozzi's doctrines and methods. For ten years
Mr. Alcott pursued the itinerant occupation of
peddler of small wares and subscription books.
He began his career as a teacher in Connecticut
in 1823, an occupation which he continued to
follow for more than fifteen years. He taught
first a district school at Bristol and in 1825 he took
charge of the school at Cheshire. Before this
date, remarked Mr. Frank B. Sanborn, in an address at the centennial celebration of the town of
Wolcott, Connecticut in 1873: "The district
schools of Connecticut, and of all New England,
were at a low grade of discipline, instruction and
comfort; and in all these matters, Mr. Alcott set
the example of improvement. He first gave his
pupils single desks, now so common, instead of

the long benches and double or three-seated desks, still in use in some sections. He gave his youthful pupils slates and pencils and blackboards. He established a school library, and taught them to enjoy the benefits of careful reading; he broke away from the old rule of severe and indiscriminate punishments and substituted therefore appeals to the affections and moral sentiments of children, so that he was able almost wholly to dispense with corporal punishment. He introduced also light gymnastic exercises, evening amusements at the school room, the keeping of diaries by young children; and, in general, an affectionate and reverant mode of drawing out the child's mind toward knowledge, rather than the pouring in of instruction by mechanical or compulsory processes. Familiar as this natural system has since become, it was an innovation five and forty years ago,—as much so as Pestalozzi's method had been in Europe when he began the instruction of poor children in Switzerland a hundred years ago."

In the *American Journal of Education* for January and February 1827, Mr. Alcott, at the request of the editor, gives an account of the organization and methods of his Cheshire school. Mr. Alcott's purpose, as there stated, is distinctly Pestalozzian. Of his course of study he says, "It is adapted professedly to the wants and genius of the young mind; it refers to children; and it is insisted that children are the best judges of what meets their views and feelings." His scheme of moral education is the most rational and the most elaborate in the annals of early American education. He quotes Pestalozzi as saying that "the only solid and true foundation of all morality is laid in the first relations of instructor and pupil," and this relation he regards as fundamental in all moral education. Equally important is the Cheshire scheme of physical education. It aims to train the physical powers in relation to the practical uses of life, and in proportion to their respective utility. It provides special exercises for the training of the eye, the ear, the hand, and the voice; and emphasis is placed on play-games such as balancing, jumping, hopping, swinging, and running. He grounds intellectual education upon the following principles: Follow nature; employ the known to induce the unknown; teach by visible and tangible objects, by oral and illustrative and familiar methods; bring all the powers of the mind into harmonious development and exercise; prepare the mind to investigate for itself, forming good mental habits, strengthening its powers by exercise, and preserving it from implicit belief; develop reason as rapidly as possible; never lose sight of the relation of cause and effect; make experiment the test of theory and the basis of fact; consult the minds, genius, and habits of the pupils; furnish constant employment. After more than three quarters of a century, how distinctly modern these principles of intellectual education sound!

Amusements constituted an important educational factor in the Cheshire school. These, argued Mr. Alcott, exercise a good influence on the affections and passions of the pupils, and improve and elevate their minds. Evening recreations at the instructor's room are provided "in which he engages himself," story telling, plays and games. The school was placed on a basis of self government, and the governing officers—a "superintendent, recorder, librarian and conservator"—co-operated with the instructor. One of the eighteen laws of the self-governing basis was: "that they behave to their companions as they desired their companions to behave to them."

Samuel J. May (1797-1871), afterwards principal of the Framingham normal school, says that he learned of the Cheshire school through Bronson Alcott's cousin Dr. William A. Alcott; "his account," continues Mr. May's autobiography, "excited so much my curiosity to know more of the American Pestalozzi, as he has since been called, that I wrote immediately to Mr. Alcott, begging him to send me a more detailed statement of his principles and methods of training children. In due time came to me a full account

of the school at Cheshire, which revealed such a
depth of insight into the nature of man, such a
true sympathy with children, such profound appreciation of the work of education, and was,
withal, so philosophically arranged and exquisitely
written, that I at once felt assured the man must
be a genius, and I must know him more intimately. So I wrote, inviting him urgently to
visit me. He came and passed a week with me
before the end of the summer. I have never, but
in one instance, been so immediately taken possession of by any man I ever met in my life. He
seemed to me like a born sage and saint. He
was a radical in all matters of reform; went to
the root of all theories, especially the subject of
education, mental and moral culture."

Reforms so pronounced as those introduced by
Mr. Alcott were not to pass unchallenged. He
met with no end of opposition, not only from the
patrons of his district but from his colleagues;
and in May 1827 he wrote: "The continuance of
the school is precarious, depending in a consider-

able degree upon the unsettled humor of the district. It may not long be continued under present superintendence. The opposing few are still awake to carry on their designs; they may succeed, having recently erected another school under the instruction of an instructress, whose pupils amount to about fifteen, leaving nearly thirty in attendance at the usual place. Time must determine the result of this proceeding. Should opposition put on an angry aspect, the original school will be relinquished. The common sentiment in the village is sufficiently improved to make something valuable to grow out of what has been attempted—come of the school what may."

In 1828 Mr. Alcott removed to Boston where he opened first an infant school and later a private school, during which time he wrote and published his *Observations on the principles and methods of infant instruction*. He was called to Philadelphia in 1830 to accept a position in a school directed by his friend William Russell. In September 1834

he returned to Boston and opened his famous
Temple school, where for a period of five years he
worked out even greater educational reforms than
he had been able to accomplish at Cheshire, the
school being of private rather than public nature.
Two women, who afterwards became distinguished
in American education and letters, were assistant
teachers in the Temple school under Mr. Alcott's
direction—Elizabeth Palmer Peabody (1804-1894)
and Sarah Margaret Fuller, afterwards the
Marchioness d'Ossoli (1810-1850). Mr. Alcott's
labors and methods at the Temple school have
been admirably presented in Miss Peabody's book
*Record of Mr. Alcott's school exemplifying the prin-
ciples and methods of moral culture* published at
Boston in 1835. Mr. Alcott's daughter Louisa
May Alcott in her *Little men* utilized many of the
incidents in the Temple school in her imaginary
Plumfield school. Miss Peabody's *Record* is
still obtainable and should be read by every student of the history of American education.
Every department of the Temple school was per-

meated by the Pestalozzian spirit. In 1836 Mr. Alcott published the first volume of his *Conversations with children on the Gospels* and a year later the second volume. This work, Mr. Sanborn says, "caused such a commotion in Boston that it led eventually to the downfall of the Temple school."

Harriet Martineau after her return to England from America in 1837 published an account of the school which was not intended to be complimentary to Mr. Alcott. She had interpreted his Pestalozzianism by stiff and mechanical English standards. James Pierrepont Greaves, an English philanthropist and disciple, saw in Miss Martineau's "intemperate tirade," the genuine Pestalozzian spirit and method and he recognized Alcott's right of succession to the Swiss reformer. He opened correspondence at once with Alcott; cordially invited him to England, and in founding his English Pestalozzian school at Ham he named it Alcott House, in honor of the American teacher. Alcott and Greaves unfortunately never met, for the latter had died a few months before the ar-

rival of Alcott in England in the early summer of
1842.

Mr. Alcott's Boston experiment, while it received the hearty approval of such well known
educators as William Russell, Henry Barnard,
Thomas Gallaudet, Ralph Waldo Emerson, Walter R. Johnson, and William Ellery Channing,
met with no end of opposition from conservative
and traditional schoolmen.   The newspapers also
attacked severely his *Conversations with children
on the gospels*.   "The effect of such denunciation,"
says Mr. Sanborn, "was crushing."   The school at
the Temple, which began in 1834 with thirty
pupils, and had received as many as forty pupils,
fell to ten in the spring of 1837, and after lingering
along for a year or two, with one or two changes
of place, was finally given up in 1839.   The immediate occasion of closing it was the unwil-
lingness of Mr. Alcott's patrons to have their children educated in the same room with a colored
child whom he had admitted; and when the pro-
testing parents found Mr. Alcott determined not

to dismiss the colored child, they withdrew their own children, leaving him with only five pupils, —his own three daughters, a child of Mr. William Russell, and young Robinson, the cause of offence.

Having devoted ten years to the occupation of clerk in a book store and itinerant peddler, and nearly sixteen years to school-keeping, Mr. Alcott consecrated the last fifty years of his long life to the study and teaching of philosophy. Concerning his educational career, Mr. Sanborn says, "As will be seen in the records of his schools at Cheshire, Philadelphia, and Boston, Alcott, like Pestalozzi, was constantly at a disadvantage in dealing with affairs; nor was he so fortunate as to find a co-adjutor who could supply the practical ability to match and complete his own idealism. Hence the brief term of his success in every place where he taught, and his frequent removals from town to town and state to state. But the best men and women everywhere aided his plans, rejoiced in his success, and knew how to pardon his failures."

8   *Lowell Mason*

The labors of Mr. Woodbridge in behalf of Pestalozzian methods of teaching vocal music were finally taken up by Lowell Mason (1792-1872), through whose vigorous efforts not only the Pestalozzian system but the cause of music in general received a most notable up-lift. Indeed, Mr. Mason is the most distinguished public school music educator yet produced by the United States. After an experience of more than eighteen years as a teacher of vocal and instrumental music, an event occurred which changed his whole manner of teaching, as well as his theory of the educational value of music. This was his meeting with Mr. Woodbridge and his introduction to the system and methods of Pestalozzi.

"For this clearer light on the subject of music education," says Henry Barnard, "Mason was indebted to the enlightened zeal, energy and perseverance in all educational improvement to the late William C. Woodbridge, so extensively known, not only as a geographer but as an edu-

cator, whose labors in both capacities mark one
of the prominent eras in the history of education
in the United States. Mr. Woodbridge while
in Germany and Switzerland, where he had resided several years, with a view of obtaining the
best methods of instruction, although like Pestalozzi, he had given little personal attention to the
subject of music, became, from his own observation of its excellent influence on the pupils of the
Pestalozzian schools in general, and especially
in the institution of Fellenberg at Hofwyl, thoroughly convinced of its importance as a school
exercise and an educational influence. He accordingly procured all the information in his
power respecting it, and obtained the most ap-
proved text-books of school or class voice-exer-
cises and songs, as well as of elementary treatises
on musical instruction. * * * These books
by Nägeli and others, which had been prepared
with particular reference to the legitimate influence of song in moral culture and the training of
the affections, Mr. Woodbridge not only placed

in the hands of Lowell Mason, but he was at trouble to translate them himself, in part, and to furnish such explanations and directions as he had received personally from Pfeiffer, Nägeli, Krüsi, Fellenberg, Kubler, Gresbach, and others.''

A wider and more important field now opened before Mr. Mason.   For a number of years he had taught gratuitously two afternoons each week children from the public schools of Boston.   With the adoption of the Pestalozzian system, the size of his juvenile classes increased enormously; and with these large classes he was able to give a series of public demonstrations of the new method in music.   He had been president of the Handel and Haydn Society since 1827, but in 1832 he declined further service that he might give his entire time to his efforts to teach vocal music to young children.   He relinquished a lucrative situation to devote his entire time to the instruction of these juvenile classes. George James Webb (1803-1887) co-operated with Mr. Mason in the direction of these classes and in the instruction given in the

Boston Academy of Music which Mr. Mason had organized.

Through Mr. Mason's efforts vocal music was introduced into the Mount Vernon School, then conducted by Jacob Abbott (1803-1879), in the Chauncy Hall School, conducted by Gideon F. Thayer (1793-1863) and in the Boston Monotorial School conducted by William B. Fowle (1795-1863). In an article in the *American Annals of Education* for May 1835, Mr. Fowle tells of the extraordinary progress made by the pupils in his school with two lessons a work of one hour each under Mr. Mason's direction; and he argues that the pupils make corresponding progress in other studies as well as in music. The success of such instruction in these schools, as well as the demonstrated results at the numerous public concerts given by Mason's juvenile classes at the Academy of Music in Boston, not only removed all prejudices against the study of vocal music in the public schools, but led the Boston school committee, in September 1836, on petition from many citizens, to authorize such study in the public schools of the city. The city council, however, failed to make the necessary appropriation; but as Mr. Mason was more interested in the educational value of the study of vocal music than in any pecuniary remuneration that might come to him for his labors, he proposed to the city to teach one school for a year free of charge and to furnish the necessary music books and materials at his own expense. The offer was accepted and for two years he contributed his service to a cause in which he was so keenly interested.

In 1838 the study was formally introduced and Lowell Mason was elected music director; for it was clearly demonstrated that the pupils in the schools where vocal music had been taught were further advanced at the end of the year in their other studies than were the pupils in the schools where music had not been taught. "Thus," remarks Mr. Mathews in his *Hundred years of music in America*, "in Lowell Mason's labors were founded the germinating principles of a national musical intelligence and knowledge, and afforded a soil upon which all higher musical culture has been founded. The desire for musical advancement thus established, and the capacity created for appreciation of the higher mission of the art, has been the fallow field in which all subsequent endeavor has been rooted."

The labors of Lowell Mason in Boston did not escape the notice of Horace Mann; and from 1845 (and until Mr. Mason's removal to New York ten years later), he was regularly engaged to give instruction in vocal music at the state teachers' nstitutes and normal schools. Mr. Mann oncei said, "It is well worth walking ten miles to hear a lesson by Lowell Mason." He visited Europe twice—in 1837 and again in 1853—that he might observe the methods of music instruction in Pestalozzian schools in Switzerland and Germany. He published many text-books on music for the use of school children, as well as many collections of secular and sacred music. His most important contribution to the pedagogy of music was the

Pestalozzian music teacher, which he published
jointly with Theodore F. Seward, with illustrative
lessons by John W. Dickinson of the Westfield
normal school.

9   *Henry Barnard*

During a long and varied educational career,
the late Henry Barnard (1811-1900) was an active
Pestalozzian propagandist in the United States.
He first learned, as he has since told me, of the
labors of the Swiss reformer from Dr. Eli Todd,
then an eminent alienist in charge of the Retreat
for the Insane at Hartford.   Barnard was at the
time a young collegian at Yale; but he said the
vivid descriptions of the self sacrificing labors of
Pestalozzi, as narrated by Dr. Todd, made an
abiding impression on his young mind.   This
must have been about 1828 or 1829.   In 1835
Mr. Barnard having completed both his college
course and his law studies, and having one year's
experience as a teacher in an academy in Pennsylvania, he went to Europe for a year for travel

and study. At Hofwyl, from Fellenberg and Wehrli, he became familiar with the methods of carrying out the reforms in which he had become so deeply interested from the accounts of his venerable medical friend, Dr. Todd.

When he took charge of the Connecticut school system in 1838, he endeavored to give practical shape to some of the ideas which Pestalozzi had advocated; and in October and November of the following year he organized and conducted for six weeks a teachers' institute—the first ever held in America—and here he presented to the twenty-five or thirty young men in attendance several lectures on the life and character of Pestalozzi and several lessons on his methods of teaching. In the *Connecticut Common School Journal* which he edited from 1838 to 1842 he published several articles on Pestalozzi. In 1839 he printed for distribution among the teachers of his state a twenty-four page monograph on "Pestalozzi, Franklin and Oberlin" and in 1847 he printed a pamphlet on "Pestalozzi's educational labors for the poor," and two years later a forty-eight page monograph on "Pestalozzi and his method of instruction."

In 1856 he began the publication of his monumental *American Journal of Education* (1856-1881); and in the thirty-two massive volumes of this most comprehensive encyclopædia of education, Mr. Barnard published more than a score of notable essays on Pestalozzi, including, among the translations of the Swiss reformer's own writings, one hundred chapters from *Leonard and Gertrude*, portions of *Christopher and Alice*, all of *Evening hours of a hermit*, the *Christmas eve discourse* of 1810, the *New Year's address*, 1808, the Seventy-second birthday address, a fragment of *How Gertrude teaches her children*, Pestalozzi's own account of his educational experience, and a fragment from *Paternal instructions*. In addition, he published exhaustive sketches of the life of Pestalozzi taken from the writings of von Raumer, Blochmann, Diesterweg, Woodbridge and Biber; and sketches of fifteen of Pestalozzi's associates and distinguished students, including Niederer, Krüsi, Buss, Schmid, Tobler, Ramsauer, Plamann, Nägeli, Harnisch, Zeller, von Türk, Denzel, Diesterweg, and Dinter. In 1858 Mr. Barnard collected these numerous essays and published the same in a comprehensive volume of nearly five hundred pages entitled *Pestalozzi and Pestalozzianism*. This volume, which is still to be had in the ordinary course of trade (Bardeen, Syracuse, N. Y.), continues to be the most valuable Pestalozzian handbook in the English language. But it was not only in Pestalozzian literature, but in every other department of educational thought that the self-sacrificing Henry Barnard was a pioneer; for he was the first in America to recognize that if teaching was to become a profesion, there must be a rich and scientific professional literature. No one before or since has labored more earnestly to give American education such a literature than the late Henry Barnard. He always sought the best; and the twenty-five thousand pages of his great journal stand unrivalled as the best encyclopædia of education in any language. In this he rendered the Pestalozzian movement splendid service, as he did the great educational movements connected with the names of Comenius, Rousseau, Fröbel and every other really great name in the history of education.

EDWARD AUSTIN SHELDON

CHAPTER VIII

PESTALOZZIANISM AT THE OSWEGO
NORMAL SCHOOL

Introduction from England. Educational museum at Toronto. Edward A. Sheldon. Life and training. Ragged school at Oswego. Superintendent of schools at Syracuse and Oswego. Beginnings of the Oswego training school. Labors of Miss Jones. Central ideas of the Oswego movement. Oswego a state normal school. Report of the committee of the National Teachers' Association. Influence of Oswego. Herman Krüsi, Jr. Training under his father. Teaching in England. Call to New England. Institute lectures. Connection with the New Jersey normal school. Call to Oswego. Closing years and labors. Professor Mary Sheldon Barnes: Training and career as a teacher. Contributions to methods of teaching history.

In 1828 Mr. William Maclure wrote: "For upwards of twenty years some considerable exertions have been made to introduce the [Pestalozzian] reforms in the education of children in the United States, with little or no success, until the system has been practiced for the last two or three years by old mother Britain; since which, it has spread considerably, under various names, overt he Union." Mr. Maclure was, however, too familiar with the Pestalozzian system at its fountain head not to recognize the mixture of British Pestalozzianism with a deal of mechanism and routine from the practices of Lancaster and Wilderspin, and this he lamented.

The phase of Pestalozzianism with which the Oswego movement has been so intimately identified is object-teaching—the Anschauungsunterricht of Pestalozzi. This movement was introduced from England—chiefly from the Home and Colonial School Society—and rather indirectly through Canada. Adolphus Egerton Ryerson (1803-1882), who was the moving spirit in the establishment of an efficient system of public instruction in the Province of Ontario, made several trips to Europe for the collection of materials for the establishment of an educational museum; and he brought to Toronto many of

the pictures, models, objects and appliances used
by the Home and Colonial School Society in their .
Pestalozzian schools in England. These materials
furnished the point of departure for Mr. Sheldon.

1 *Edward A. Sheldon*

Edward Austin Sheldon, who was born at
Perry Center, Wyoming county, New York, on the
4th of October, 1823, received his elementary
training in the common schools and his college
preparation in a near-by academy. He entered
Hamilton College intending to fit himself for the
profession of law. His health broke and he was
forced to leave college at the close of his junior
year. Shortly after leaving college he was
brought face to face with the ignorance and misery
of the poor living at Oswego where he had located
for the purpose of engaging in business. "Day
after day," writes his daughter, the late Professor
Mary Sheldon Barnes, "he went through tene-
ment houses and shanties, learning to know the
miseries and wants of their inmates; armed with

a little book full of statistics he himself had gathered, with his fresh young heart urging on to
action, he persuaded some of his most influential
friends to join him in forming an Orphan and
Free School Association, which should find some
way of giving a home to the orphans and a free
school to the poorer children of Oswego.   *   *   *
Active results soon appeared, and a room was
rented and fitted for a school.   But who should
be the teacher?   To his own utter surprise every-
one turned to my father as a matter of course.
He had just completed arrangements for entering
the theological seminary at Auburn; but since no
teacher appeared, and his associates declared
that unless he would teach the school they would
abandon the enterprise, he answered, trusting
still to the lead of Providence, 'Very well, then
teach the school I must.'   When asked what
salary he wanted, he said, 'It will cost me about
$275 a year to live and this is all I want.'   They
gave him $300 and my father entered what after-
wards proved his own chosen career.''

This was in the late autumn of 1848. The "Ragged School," for such it was called, was composed in the main of one hundred and twenty rude and untrained Irish boys and girls between the ages of five and twenty-one years. Yet, adds his daughter, they gave him no trouble. If they engaged in a free fight, it was from ignorance of the proprieties of the time and place, not from any desire to be ugly; if some of the boys became restless, they were sent out to race around the block and see who could be back first; they were called to order by rapping on the stovepipe; they were held in order and kept to their work by the genuine love they bore their young schoolmaster and by the genuine love he bore them. "As my father went to work of a morning," she writes, "his warm-hearted Irish children trooped about him, seizing him by the fingers or the coat-tails, wherever they could best catch hold, to the great amusement of the storekeepers and the passers-by. Saturday morning he spent in pastoral work, that is, in visiting his pupils at home, and in seeing that they were not suffering from the necessities of life.   This was the hardest day of his week; and the young schoolmaster generally found himself exhausted by noon, so great was the draft made on his sympathies by ignorance, sickness, incompetence, and misfortune." Truly, here was manifested the spirit of Pestalozzi; and how well this account tallies with the latter's labors among the poor and the neglected at Neuhof and Stanz!*

Out of this philanthropic movement grew the free and graded schools of Oswego.   Mr. Sheldon was superintendent of the schools of Syracuse from 1851 to 1853 when he returned again to Oswego—this time to organize a free public school system in which poor and rich alike were received on equal footing.   "His sincere and thoughtful

---

*Neuhof, the scenes of Pestalozzi's first educational efforts (1775–1780), is a small rural village near Zurich.   Stanz is a town on the southern shores of Lake Lucerne in the secluded valley of Nidwalden where he conducted an orphanage for two years (1798–1799).

nature," writes Mrs. Barnes, "had become dissatisfied, not only with the current ways of teaching in our public schools, but even with their range of subjects. His early life on the farm, his taste for practical work, his sympathetic contact with the poor, had convinced him that something better and more useful could be done in the way of education. He felt that children should learn to know forms, colors, weights, the commoner facts and relations of their own bodies and the material world—not as mere names, but as objective realities. While working the problem over, he visited Toronto, where he saw in the National [Educational] Museum, though not used in their own schools, collections of appliances employed abroad—notably in the Home and Colonial Training School in London."

This was during the early part of the year 1860. With such teaching appliances as he was able to import from London, Mr. Sheldon began the reorganization of the schools of Oswego with special reference to object teaching as the core of the

system.   He met with his teachers on Saturdays
and instructed them in the new methods to the
best of his ability; and in his report for that year
he wrote: "The system which we have adopted
is justly termed Pestalozzian, for to Pestalozzi,
that greatest of all modern reformers in education, may be credited the development and in
many important points the origin of those ideas
which lie at the basis of this system.   It is true
that these ideas, and the modes of applying them
in the development of the human faculties, have
been somewhat modified and improved during
the experience of half a century, but they are
none the less the real thoughts and discoveries
of this great philosopher.   Its principles have
become more or less widely diffused, but have
been more generally and thoroughly incorporated
with the methods of teaching in some of the countries of Europe, than in our own.   Especially is
this true of Germany, Switzerland, Prussia and
France.   But in no country, perhaps, have these
principles been more thoroughly systematized

and developed than in a few training colleges in Great Britain."

After the system had been on trial for a year, it was decided to send to London and engage a Pestalozzian teacher to come to Oswego and organize a training class. "It is to be a kind of practicing school," said the Oswego school report for that year, "where beginners serve their apprenticeship. In many mechanical trades, years of toilsome apprenticeship have to be served out before the artisan is trusted alone with his tools. If, then, such great care is taken to prepare him for his work who has to form the senseless block of wood or marble into lines and forms of beauty, how much more—infinitely more, important is it, that he who has to mould and give form and symmetry to the immortal soul, should make some preparation for his work; should at least receive some hints and suggestions from a master's hand. He ought also to have some understanding of his subject, as well as the tools he is to use, and the best method of using them. Pupils are expected to spend one year in observation and practice in this school before receiving an appointment to teach in our city schools.   At least one half of each day is to be spent in this way, and the other portion in study and recitation in those branches of natural history and mental science of immediate importance in connection with this system of instruction.   Two hours each day will also be devoted to instruction in methods of teaching. Primary School No. 4 has been selected for this Model School.   There are accommodations here for three pupil teachers to be engaged in practice at the same time."

Margaret E. M. Jones (1824-   ), for fifteen years connected with the Home and Colonial Training School at Gray's Inn Road, London, came to Oswego, May the 1st, 1861, and began her labors as a training teacher.   "Her teaching," wrote the late Herman Krüsi, Jr., "was essentially based on principles which owe their chief advocacy and practical application to the work of the Swiss school reformer, Pestalozzi.   The more exclusive attention to object lessons, as a separate branch of study, was of English origin, and has since been greatly modified. Yet it was this new feature in particular which struck casual observers as worthy of attention and imitation.''

The central ideas of the new system, as stated by the Oswego authorities in 1861, were (1) That all education should be according to the natural order of development of the human faculties; (2) that all knowledge is derived in the first instance from the perceptions of the senses, and therefore that all instruction should be based upon real objects and occurrences; (3) that the object of primary education is to give a harmonious cultivation to the faculties of the mind, and not to communicate technical knowledge. These were the principles upon which Mr. Sheldon based his innovations. It is needless to say that the Oswego reforms soon met the ill-concealed hostility of the advocates of the old order, many of whom knew little of the workings of the new system and practically nothing of its basic principles. Accord-

ingly, in December 1861, Mr. Sheldon, through
the Oswego board of education, issued an invita-
tion to certain leading educators of the country
to come to Oswego and look into the nature of
the new work.   William F. Phelps, D. H. Cochran,
David N. Camp, Thomas F. Harrison, H. P.
Wilbur, George L. Farnham and W. Nicoll constituted the special committee of the invited
educators.   They spent the 11th, 12th and 13th
of February, 1862, at Oswego, in a careful examination of the new system and in listening to two
papers on the Pestalozzian system, the first, "The
laws of childhood" by Miss M. E. M. Jones, and
the second, "The history of object teaching" by
Norman A. Calkins.   *Barnard's American Journal
of Education* for 1863 (vol. 12, pp. 605-646) published a full report of the findings of the committee
and the papers by Miss Jones and Mr. Calkins.
The committee after due deliberation concluded
that the principles of the Pestalozzian system
were philosophical and sound and in harmony
with the nature of man ; that the particular meth-

ods of instruction presented before them at Oswego as illustrative of those principles merit and
receive hearty approbation, subject to such mod-
ifications as experience and the characteristics
of our people may determine to be wise and ex-
pedient; and recommended the adoption of the
system in whole or in part wherever such introduction was practicable. The committee recognized that the system to a great measure elimi-
nated books from the primary schools—or, as they
stated it, "the system substitutes in great measure
teachers for the book"—and they recognized in
consequence that attempts to introduce it by
those not clearly comprehending its principles,
and not trained in its methods, would result only
in failure.

In 1863, Victor Moreau Rice (1818-1869), then
state superintendent of public instruction in New
York, became interested in the Pestalozzian
movement at Oswego, and he secured an annual
grant from the state of three thousand dollars
toward the support of the school for a period of

two years; and in 1866 Oswego became one of
the regular state normal schools of New York.
At the fourth annual meeting of the National
Teachers' Association held at Chicago in August
1863 Mr. Sheldon read a paper on object teaching
which elicited such wide-spread comment that at
the meeting held at Ogdensburg a year later a
committee was appointed to investigate the principles of object teaching in general and the Oswego
system in particular. The committee included
Barnas Sears (1802-1880), then president of
Brown university and formerly secretary of the
state board of education in Massachusetts;
Samuel Stillman Greene (1810-1883), professor
in Brown University; Josiah Little Pickard (1824
-    ), superintendent of schools at Chicago;
John Dudley Philbrick (1818-1886), superintendent of schools at Boston; David N. Camp (1820-
    ), superintendent of the schools of Connecti-
cut; Richard Edwards (1822-   ), principal of
the Illinois state normal school, and C. L. Pennell
of St. Louis. The report was drawn up by Mr.

Greene and presented at the fifth annual meeting of the National Teachers' Association held at Harrisburg in August 1865.

The committee sought to investigate three questions touching the problem of object teaching: 1. What place do external objects hold in the acquisition of knowledge? Are they the exclusive source of our knowledge? 2. So far as our knowledge is obtained from external objects as a source, how far can any educational processes facilitate the process? 3. Are the measures adopted at Oswego in accordance with the general principles resulting from these inquiries? The report covers twenty-five pages; and, while Mr. Pennell is reported as somewhat adverse to anything like systematic object teaching, the other six members of the committee heartily commend the system. "Whenever this system has been confined to elementary instruction," reports the committee, "and has been employed by skillful, thorough teachers, in unfolding and disciplining the faculties, in fixing the attention and awakening thought, it has been successful. Pupils trained under this system have evinced more quickness and accuracy of perception, careful observation, and a correctness of judgment which results from accurate discrimination, and proper comparison. They have seemed much better acquainted with the works of nature, and better able to understand allusions to nature, art, and social life." The committee took occasion, however, to warn against object lessons supplanting the use of books in higher instruction.

From the Oswego normal school the phase of Pestalozzianism, with which this institution was directly interested, spread throughout the country through the students trained under Mr. Sheldon, Mr. Krüsi and a long list of worthy associates. Hence the school and its earnest disciples of the great Pestalozzi warrant large recognition at the hands of the historian of the Pestalozzian movement in the United States. Mr. Sheldon, it should be noted in this connection, continued at the head

H. Krüsi

of the Oswego normal school until the time of his
death, August the 28th, 1897.

2 *Herman Krüsi, Jr.*

Miss Jones' labors at Oswego ended in the summer of 1862, but the work of the training school
was continued by Herman Krüsi, Jr., and teachers
who had been her pupils.   From this time, Mr.
Krüsi, after Mr. Sheldon, became the most notable
figure in the Oswego movement.   Mr. Krüsi was
born at Yverdon, Switzerland, June 24th 1817.
His father had been for many years, both at
Burgdorf and Yverdon, Pestalozzi's chief assistant.   He received his elementary education in the
Canton of Appenzel and he subsequently entered
the normal school at Gais, where his father was
principal.   After completing the course of instruction he continued for three years his studies
in the German normal schools at Dresden and
Berlin.   Returning to Gais in 1838 he accepted a
position in the normal school under his father

which he continued to fill until the latter's death in 1846.

In 1846 he received an appointment in the Pestalozzian school at Cheam, England, conducted by Charles Mayo. The school was patronized chiefly by the wealthy classes and the nobility, and the method of teaching employed there, notes Krüsi, was the old routine system which was very distasteful to him. On leaving Cheam he received an appointment in the training school conducted by the Home and Colonial School Society. This school he found more distinctly Pestalozzian than the one at Cheam. He had charge of the classes in drawing and mathematics; and here he worked out his system of inventive drawing. He returned to Switzerland in 1852 intending to engage in educational work in his native country; but he chanced to meet Lowell Mason on one of his trips to Europe to study the Pestalozzian system and Mr. Mason had cordially recommended Krüsi to William Russell, then requiring the service of an additional teacher in his private normal school at Lancaster, Massachusetts. "This gave him an opportunity to realize one of his cherished dreams—to visit America—and in 1852 he again left his mountain home to begin work in a new land." Mr. Krüsi has himself told me that he had formed a strong desire to come to America after reading the reports of the state board of education of Massachusetts by Horace Mann. These reports he had found in the library of the Home and Colonial School Society in London.

Mr. Krüsi continued in Mr. Russell's school as teacher of drawing and modern languages for five years; and in the meantime he was employed by the state board of education of Massachusetts to give instruction to the teachers of the commonwealth at state institutes on methods of teaching arithmetic and drawing. He had as associates in the Massachusetts institutes two of his countrymen Louis Aagassiz (1807-1873) and Arnold Guyot (1807-1884); also William Russell (1798-1873), Lowell Mason (1792-1872), George Barrell

Emerson (1797-1881) and other well known New England school men. In 1853 Mr. Krüsi presented to the American Institute of Instruction at New Haven an important essay on the educational labors of Pestalozzi, which led Yale college to confer upon him the honorary degree of Master of Arts. Mr. Krüsi's associates in the normal school at Lancaster, besides Mr. Russell, were: William J. Whitaker, who had been his colleague in the Home and Colonial Training College at London, Sanborn Tenny, the naturalist, who was afterwards for many years a professor at Amherst College, and Dana Pond Colburn, who was subsequently principal of the state normal school at Providence, Rhode Island.

The organization of state normal schools in Massachusetts, and the liberal course adopted by the commonwealth in establishing scholarships at her colleges for the benefit of young men intending to prepare themselves for the work of teaching, made unnecessary a private teachers' seminary of the nature of Mr. Russell's, and it

was accordingly abolished in 1857. Two years
before, William Franklin Phelps (1822—   ) had
organized the state normal school at Trenton,
New Jersey; and learning that Mr. Krüsi was
free, he engaged him as an instructor in his school.
After two years at Trenton Mr. Krüsi returned to
Massachusetts and for three years he gave his
whole time to the work of instructing teachers at
institutes in Massachusetts and the other New
England states.   In 1862, as before pointed out,
Mr. Krüsi was engaged by Mr. Sheldon for the
Oswego normal school, and for a period of twenty-
five years he taught with great earnestness and intelligence the Pestalozzian system of education to
thousands of prospective teachers who graduated
from the Oswego normal school during this important period of the school's history.   He first
taught methods of number, form and drawing
and superintended the practice teaching in the
training school, as well as in the public schools of
the city.   Later he taught the philosophy and
history of education, as well as mental and moral

philosophy; and while here he prepared and published his valuable work on the life, principles,
and character of Pestalozzi.   After a quarter of a
century at Oswego he resigned his position in the
school and passed his closing years with his son
at Alameda, California, where he died January
28th 1902.   Like the great Pestalozzi, Mr. Krüsi
had the simplicity of a child.   One of his students
says of his teaching: "His manner of presentation
was clear and logical, but withal charmingly
frank, and a genial humor constantly played about
the topic of the hour."

3   *Mary Sheldon Barnes*

A large and permanent contribution of the
Oswego movement to the science of education
was the application of Pestalozzian principles to
the teaching of history.   Mr. Sheldon's daughter,
Professor Mary Sheldon Barnes (1850-1898), did
for the teaching of history what Karl Ritter and
Hennig had done for the teaching of geography—
she applied the inductive method to the develop-

ment of local historic concepts and the gradual up-building of the historic sense by means of objective materials having a visible connection with the past. After her graduation from the Oswego normal school, Miss Sheldon entered the University of Michigan where she graduated in 1874. She taught for two years in the Oswego normal school and in 1876 she accepted an appointment as professor of history in Wellesley College, which position she filled for four years. During 1880 to 1882 she travelled and studied in Europe; and upon her return she accepted an appointment of instructor of history in the Oswego normal school.

She married Professor Earl Barnes in 1884; and during the next seven years she was engaged chiefly in study, travel, and literary work. In 1891 both she and her husband were appointed professors in Stanford University—she in the department of modern history and he in the department of education. Mrs. Barnes was the first woman to receive appointment in the faculty of Stanford University. In an institution where all the courses of instruction were elective, and where more than two thirds of the students were of the male sex, Mrs. Barnes enrolled in her first course of lectures at Stanford University one hundred students, eighty percent. of whom were men. She was so thoroughly in possession of her subject matter and such a master of the method which she employed that few, if any, surpassed her in the department of history.

In the province of history-teaching from sources, Professor Mary Sheldon Barnes was a pioneer; and although this method is now very generally employed in most higher institutions of learning in America, and in many secondary schools, it should not be forgotten that the method was not only not in use, but that it was entirely unknown in the United States when Mary Sheldon began the use of the method in the Oswego normal school thirty-two years ago. Her *Studies in general history*, with the teachers' manuals accompanying the same, and her *Studies in the historical method*, give the pedagogic basis of her method.   It was

Mrs. Barnes who first brought American students into a living, thoughtful relation with historical realities; and her development of the laboratory method in the study of history has been as important for the furtherance of Pestalozzianism as similar developments in geography by Ritter and Hennig.

CHAPTER IX

WILLIAM T. HARRIS AND PESTALOZZIANISM IN THE SCHOOLS OF ST. LOUIS

Training and early educational labors of William T. Harris. Election to the superintendency of the schools of St. Louis. His professional equipment as characterized by Henry Barnard. Study of natural science in the schools. Criticism and discussion of Pestalozzian doctrines and methods.

Much of the Pestalozzian method (and more of the Pestalozzian spirit) characterized the administration of the schools of St. Louis from 1868 to 1880. It was during this period that St. Louis became generally known as possessing the best supervised and the most wisely directed common school system of the world; and the twelve annual reports prepared by its superintendent have taken classic rank in the literature of city school administration.

William Torrey Harris (1835–   ), who was superintendent of the public schools of St. Louis

1868 to 1880, has always stood for all that was best in the Pestalozzian system. He was educated in the district schools of Windham County, Connecticut, the grammar schools of Providence, the academies at Woodstock, Worcester, and Andover, and at Yale College. After a varied experience as a teacher in the elementary schools of New England, Mr. Harris located in St. Louis in 1858. He was first an assistant teacher in the Franklin school and was shortly made principal of the Clay school. In 1866 he was selected as assistant superintendent of the schools of the city; and two years later he was promoted to the superintendency. This post he held until 1880, when, to the great regret of all interested in the educational welfare of St. Louis, he signified his purpose to withdraw from the work.

Concerning the eminent educational fitness of Mr. Harris for the supervision of the schools of a great city, the late Henry Barnard wrote: "It is seldom that a school officer enters on the administration of a system with such practical knowledge of all the details which enter into the studies, the first admission, the successive promotions from grade to grade, and the instruction from the primary class to the high and normal school. To this practical experience of his own, he was constantly adding a diligent study of the best treatises in the English, French, and German languages on the general principles of education and the organization and administration of systems of public instruction; and at the same time, Mr. Harris was subjecting his own experience and views, and the experience of others gathered from books, to the experience and discussions of living teachers and school officers assembled in city, state, and national conventions." When Mr. Harris resigned from the superintendency of the St. Louis schools in 1880, to seek rest for a time in foreign travel, diversified observation, and literary work, Mr. Barnard said in his *American Journal of Education*, "Seldom has any school officer received such unequivocal evidence that his labors were properly appre-

ciated in quarters where the best judgment could
be formed from a full knowledge of his methods
and their results."

It is not the purpose of the present chapter to
trace the diversified character and the vital nature
of the reforms worked out by Mr. Harris in St.
Louis from 1868 to 1880, such as the incorporation of the kindergarten into the public school
system, the addition of German instruction in
the elementary grades without the diminution of
instruction in English, and closer supervision
and more frequent promotion of pupils; but to
discuss briefly the introduction of natural science
into the schools of St. Louis and to sum-
marize the discussion of Pestalozzianism in his
annual reports.

The Anschauungsunterricht of Pestalozzi and
the object teaching of Mr. Sheldon took the form
of natural science at St. Louis. As indicated in
one of his annual reports, "In order to adapt the
course of study to the wants of a manufacturing
community (an office which the kindergarten also

assists in performing), and to the general demands of the age, the study of natural science has been introduced into all grades of the district schools. Oral lessons are given one day in the week, one hour, in length, and as the course is a spiral one, it is traversed anew once in three years each pupil has the opportunity of coming to the same topics three times in his course through the district schools."

In the first school year instruction was given in botany; the first quarter, in flowers, their structure, color, perfume, habits, and shapes; the second quarter, leaves, fruits, and seeds, their shape, uses, sap, and decay; the third quarter, buds and roots, stalks and trunks, bark of plants and wood; fourth quarter, circulation of sap, what is made from sap, sleep of plants and re-view of the topics of the year. Animal study, with special reference to physiology, was taken up the second school year; the elements of physical nature—air, wind, water and gravitation,—were studied the third school year; and during the

fourth and fifth years botany, zoölogy, physiology and hygiene were more fully and more system-
atically studied; physical geography was introduced the sixth year and elementary physics
the seventh year.

The general introduction of natural science in
the elementary schools of St. Louis attracted
wide-spread attention throughout the country
and led shortly to the incorporation of nature
study, in one form or another, into most of the
common schools of the United States. The first
discussion of the educational value of natural
science appeared in the report of the schools of
St. Louis for 1871; and a fuller discussion followed
in the report for 1877. The syllabus of lessons
on natural science, which he prepared for the use
of the teachers of his city, was widely reprinted
by the school superintendents of the country;
and it has now become one of the classics in the
movement of science teaching in the elementary
schools of the United States.*

*Dr. Harris's report on this subject is published as a separ-

In his first annual report of the schools of St. Louis (1867-8) Mr. Harris discusses with characteristic force the pedagogic basis of Pestalozzianism, and gives his own viewpoint on the problem of object teaching. He notes that "Pestalozzi lived at a time when all Europe was done to death with formalism, and the time was preparing slowly and surely to burn up in one vast conflagration all these worn out costumes in which empty pretension still strutted about and seemed to direct. The French revolution (and the Napoleonic thirty years' war) was at hand. Rousseau had lifted up his voice and proclaimed Nature. Let us all go back to a state of nature and free ourselves from these irksome constraints that society has imposed upon us. * * * Pestalozzi began with the intention to elevate the natural over the spiritual; to dissolve the subject into the object rather than the contrary. He virtually inverted his theory and builded ' better

ate volume: *How to teach natural science in public schools*, C. W. Bardeen, Syracuse, 1895.

than he knew'. " It was a virtue of the St. Louis application of nature study that it was not given the one-sided emphasis on sense-perception so often urged by advocates of object-teaching and the Pestalozzian doctrine. While recognizing all that was of distinct educational value in the system, Mr. Harris was not blind to the faults in Pestalozzi's theory.

He has also called attention to the question whether a premature and exclusive training of sense-perception will not produce an animal plane of intelligence of the human mind, something like what is called arrested development; for, as he has pointed out, "the psychologist soon discovers that the power of thinking (both analytical and synthetical) is not a continued and elevated sort of sense-perception, but rather a reaction against it, which is negative toward the impressions and images of sense. The element of thought is generalization, and this deals with definitions rather than with images or pictures of sense. Instead of reproducing the things of experience, the thinking activity has to do with the forces, energies or causes which produce things and likewise annul and remove things by the continual process of change. In other words, thought deals with the dynamic elements of experience rather than with mere things, which are only static results. Pursuing this line of inquiry, the reader will everywhere find Pestalozzi's experiments and writings of a stimulating character, suggesting far more than they reveal, and pointing significantly toward the great educational process which is active in our time." The schools of St. Louis, under the supervision of William T. Harris, gave practical form to a phase of Pestalozzi's doctrine that has since been fruitful in making more concrete and objective the study of the world of nature.

CHAPTER X

PESTALOZZIAN LITERATURE IN THE
UNITED STATES

Mr. Maclure's earliest publications. Books by Neef. Articles in the *Academician*. Griscom's book. Articles by Woodbridge. Letters to Greaves published. Biber's life. Barnard's numerous publications. Abridged Leonard and Gertrude. Most recent Pestalozzian publications.

So far as is known, the first account of Pestalozzi's labors and doctrines, to be published in the United States, appeared in the *National Intelligencer* of Washington in the issue for June the 6th, 1806. It was based upon material furnished by William Maclure. In the issues of the 9th and 30th of the same month there appeared in the same journal translations from a work by Chavannes on the life of Pestalozzi and his methods of teaching. These translations were also made presumably by Mr. Maclure. Two years later Neef published in Philadelphia his *Sketch of a plan and method in education* which gave Americans a very clear view of the labors and methods of Pestalozzi; and in 1813 the same author published his *Method of instructing children rationally in the arts of writing and reading.*

The *Academician*, the earliest distinctly educational journal in America (1818-1819), published, in the number for January 1819, an article on Pestalozzi's method of teaching religious and moral principles to children. And in succeeding numbers—February, March, April, May and June, a reader of the *Academician*. who signed himself "A native of Clinton County [New York]" wrote a series of rather elaborate and valuable articles on Pestalozzi's life and doctrines. This contributor had not visited Yverdon, but he possessed the complete Cotta edition of Pestalozzi's writings, besides other works on the Pestalozzian method that had appeared in German and French. He speaks of the French work by Jullien and a Spanish translation of Chavannes' work. In his closing article he says: "I

possess more than thirty volumes in the German
language containing the details of the instruction which I would cheerfully give to any institution or publisher, upon the condition that they
would be translated, printed and published. And
the gift would be a free offering, nor do I wish
to be known in so doing, my only interest in obtaining those works from Europe being to pro-
mote knowledge, without any view to pecuniary
advantage." I regret that I have been unable
to learn the name of this early American disciple
of Pestalozzi.

John Griscom (1774-1852), who early became
interested in the doctrines of Pestalozzi, taught
first in a district school; was principal of the academy at Burlington, New Jersey (1794-1807);
conducted a private school of science in New
York City (1808-1818); and during the years 1818
and 1819, travelled in Europe for the purpose
of making a study of educational institutions.
He published in 1823 a two volume work which
embodied the results of his travels and observa-

tions.   Henry Barnard says of Griscom's *Year in Europe:* "No one volume in the first half of the nineteenth century had so wide an influence on the development of our educational, reformatory, and preventive measures, directly and indirectly, as this."   Griscom gives an elaborate account of his visit to Yverdon and of his impressions of Pestalozzi's method.   There were ninety boys in the school at the time—Swiss, German, French, Italian, Spanish, Russian and English—and twelve instructors.   Greaves was with Pestalozzi at the time and accompanied them on a visit to the orphanage at Clendy.   He also visited Fellenberg's institution at Hofwyl, and here he found the Pestalozzian method followed.   Griscom's thoughtful and graphic account of Pestalozzi and the institution at Yverdon was widely read in the United States and it must have been productive of good results.

William C. Woodbridge visited Pestalozzi in 1820 and again in 1825 and published several articles in the *American Journal of Education* which embodied the results of his impressions. With the establishment of the New Harmony community in 1825, many articles on Pestalozzianism appeared in the United States; but these publications have already been mentioned in the chapters treating of William Maclure and the New Harmony school.

In the *American Journal of Education* for September, 1829, William Russell began the publication of Pestalozzi's letters to Greaves on the early education of the child. These letters, strange to say, were not republished from the English edition of 1827 but were translated from a French educational journal; but the French translation was based on the English edition. These letters appeared in book form at Boston in 1830. This, so far as I know, is the earliest publication in America of any of Pestalozzi's own writings. In 1833 *Greenback's Periodical Library* of Philadelphia began the serial publication of Biber's *Life of Pestalozzi* [2], which had been published in England two years before.

Beginning with 1834, and for ten years thereafter, many American students of education—Henry Barnard, Charles Brooks, Alex. Dallas Bache, Calvin E. Stowe, Lowell Mason and Horace Mann—visited Europe and published elaborate accounts, upon their return, of the Pestalozzian movement in the old world; but the contributions of these students have already been given in the chapter treating of Pestalozzianism in New England.

After the *Letters on the early education of the child* to Greaves,[9] the next one of Pestalozzi's works to be printed in the United States was *Leonard and Gertrude*. Fragments of the same appeared in *Barnard's American Journal of Education* during 1858 and 1859; and in his comprehensive volume on *Pestalozzi and Pestalozzianism,**

*Mr. C. W. Bardeen of Syracuse, N. Y., has just brought out new and improved edition of this valuable work, giving in one volume (758 pages) all the articles on Pestalozzi and his educational system published by Dr. Barnard in his *American Journal of Education*. Besides the two portraits of Dr. Barnard, the publisher has added eighteen rare portraits

published in 1859, Mr. Barnard gave, in English translations, one hundred chapters of the pedagogical romance, together with the *Evening hours of a hermit* and several of the birthday and New Year addresses. In 1885 Miss Eva Channing published an abridged translation of *Leonard and Gertrude*[7] from the cheap Reclam edition, comprising the first two volumes only of the original. For this translation G. Stanley Hall wrote an altogether noteworthy introduction which epitomizes in less than four pages the pedagogic significance of the romance. In 1894 Mr. Bardeen brought out an American edition of the English translation of *How Gertrude teaches her children*. The translation was made by Lucy E. Holland and Frances E. Turner and the volume was excellently edited by Ebenezer Cooke. The editor's introduction and notes add great value to the worth of the translation. In 1898 Mr. Bardeen republished the first English edition

of Pestalozzi and his institution. This important work is a veritable Pestalozzian *vade mecum*.

(1827) of Pestalozzi's *Letters on early education* addressed to J. P. Greaves.

Of the lives of Pestalozzi printed in the United States, besides the republication of the not altogether trustworthy English work by Biber, to which reference has already been made, Barnard included in his *Pestalozzi and Pestalozzianism* (1859) a translation of the comprehensive sketch by Karl von Raumer. In 1875 Herman Krüsi, Jr., published his *Life, work, and influence of Pestalozzi*; and quite recently (1901) A. Pinloche has published in the Great Educator Series his *Pestalozzi and the foundation of the modern elementary school*. There are two American editions of the valuable life by Roger de Guimps; the first made by Margaret Cuthbertson Crombie, and published at Syracuse in 1889, and the second a republication of John Russell's English translation (New York, 1897).

Many so-called Pestalozzian text books have been published in this country for the use of school children—books on science, music, arith-

metic, etc., but as few of these bear the ear-
marks of familiarity with the spirit of the great
Swiss reformer's work. I have not thought
it worth while to mention them in this brief survey of the history of the Pestalozzian movement
in the United States.

CHAPTER XI.

Bibliography of the Pestalozzian Movement in the United States.

I Spread of Pestalozzianism in Europe.

1. *Barnard, Henry.*

    Pestalozzi, Fellenberg and Wehrli. *Barnard's American Journal of Education*, 1869. Vol. 21. pp. 565-576.

2. *Barnard, Henry, editor.*

    Pestalozzi and Pestalozzianism: life, educational principles and methods of John Henry Pestalozzi, with biographical sketches of several of his assistants and associates. New York, 1859. Two parts, pp. 238 and 230. Now published by C. W. Bardeen, Syracuse, N. Y.*

3. *Compayré, Gabriel.*

    History of pedagogy. Translated by W.

*See foot note on page 210.

H. Payne.   Boston, 1886.   pp. 413-445.

4. *Gill, John.*

Systems of education.   London, 1887.   pp. 48-154.

5. *de Guimps, Roger.*

Pestalozzi: his aim and work.   Translated by Margaret Cuthbertson Crombie.   Syracuse, 1889.   pp. 320.

6. *Harris, William Torrey.*

Herbart and Pestalozzi compared.   *Educational Review*, May 1893, Vol. 5.   pp. 417-423.

7. *Hughes, James Laughlin.*

Fröbel's educational laws for all teachers.   New York, 1897.   pp. 31-47.

8. *Krüsi, Herman, Jr.*

Pestalozzi: his life, work, and influence.   New York, [1875].   pp. 248.

9. *Krüsi, Herman, Sr.*

My educational recollections.   Translated by Herman Krüsi, Jr.   Barnes' Studies in

education, Vol. 1. Stanford University
1897. pp. 230-249 and 273-280.

10. *Mayo, Charles.*

Lectures on the life of Pestalozzi. London,
1856.

11. *Monroe, Paul.*

Text-book in the history of education
New York, 1905. pp. 597-624.

12. *Munroe, James Phinney.*

Educational ideal: an outline of its growth
in modern times. Boston, 1895. pp. 179-
206.

13. *Pinloche, A.*

Pestalozzi and the foundation of the modern
elementary school. New York, 1901. pp.
306.

14. *von Raumer, Karl.*

Life and system of Pestalozzi. Translated
by J. Tilleard, London, 1855.

15. *Quick, Robert Hebert.*

Essays on educational reformers. Syra-

cuse, 1900. pp. 204-252. New York, 1893.
pp. 290-383.

16. *Williams, Samuel Gardner.*

History of modern education. Syracuse,
1896. pp. 330-349.

II WILLIAM MACLURE: FIRST AMERICAN DIS-
CIPLE OF PESTALOZZI.

1. *Barnard, Henry.*

Pestalozzianism in the United States.
Barnard's American Journal of Education,
1880. Vol. 30. pp. 561-572.

2. *Griscom, John.*

A year in Europe. New York, 1823.
Two volumes. pp. 520 and 562.

3. *Maclure, William.*

An epitome of the improved Pestalozzian
system of education. *American Journal
of Science and Arts*, February, 1826. Vol.
10. pp. 145-156.

4. *Maclure, William.*

Opinions on various subjects. New Harmony, 1831. pp. 642. [Contains twenty essays on education, most of which refer to Pestalozzi].

5. *Monroe, Will Seymour.*

Joseph Neef and Pestalozzianism in America. *Education*, April, 1894. Vol. 14. pp. 479-461.

6. *Morton, Samuel George.*

A memoir of William Maclure, Esq. *American Journal of Science and Arts*, October 1844, Vol. 47. pp. 1-17.

7. *Owen, Robert.*

Life of Robert Owen. Written by himself. London, 1857. Two volumes, pp. 390 and 358.

III JOSEPH NEEF: A COADJUTOR OF PESTALOZZI.

1. *Gardette, C. D.*

Pestalozzi in America. *Galaxy*, August 1867. Vol. 4. pp. 432-439.

2. *Monroe, Will Seymour.*

Joseph Neef and Pestalozzianism in Amer-

ica. *Education,* April 1894.   Vol. 14.p.   p
449-461.

3. *Neef, Joseph.*

Sketch of a plan and method of education.
Philadelphia, 1808.   pp. 168.

4. *Pompée, Ph.*

Etudes sur la vie et les travaux de J. H.
Pestalozzi.   Paris, 1850.

5. *Ramsauer, Johann.*

Kurze Skizze meines pädagogischen Lebens
mit besonderer Berücksichtigung auf Pestalozzi und seine Anstalten. Neuburg,
1838.

6. *Wood, C. H.*

First disciple of Pestalozzi in America.
Indiana School Journal, November 1892.
Vol. 37 pp. 659-665.

IV   NEEF'S PLAN AND METHOD OF EDUCATION.

1.   *Monroe, Will Seymour.*

Pestalozzian literature in America. *Kinder-*

garten Magazine, May 1894. Vol. 6. pp. 673-676.

2. *Monroe, Will Seymour.*

Some early American books on education. *Journal of Education* (Boston) May 25th and June 8th, 1893.

3. *Neef, Joseph.*

Method of instructing children rationally in the arts of reading and writing Philadelphia, 1813. pp. 388.

4. *Neef, Joseph.*

Sketch of a plan and method of education, founded on an analysis of the human faculties and natural reason, suitable for the offspring of a free people, and for all rational beings. Philadelphia, 1808. pp. 168.

5. *Neef, Joseph*, translator.

Logic of Condillac. Philadelphia, 1809. pp. 138.

V   FIRST AMERICAN PESTALOZZIAN SCHOOL
AT PHILADELPHIA.

1. *Farragut, Loyall.*

Life of David Glasgow Farragut, embody-
ing his journals and letters.   New York,
1879.   pp. 586.

2. *Gardette, C. D.*

Pestalozzi in America.   *Galaxy*, August
1867.   Vol. 4.   pp. 432-439.

3. *Monroe, Will Seymour.*

Joseph Neef and Pestalozzianism in America.   *Education*, April 1894.   Vol 14.   pp.
449-461.

4. *Neef, Joseph.*

Sketch of a plan and method of education.
Philadelphia, 1808.   pp. 168.

5. *Wickersham, James Pyle.*

History of education in Pennsylvania.
Lancaster, 1886.   p. 484.

VI PESTALOZZIAN SCHOOL AT THE NEW HAR-
MONY COMMUNITY.

1. *Hill, G. Birbeck.*

Life of Sir Rowland Hill. London, 1880.

2. *Lockwood, George Browning.*

   New Harmony communities. Marion, (Indiana), 1902. pp. 282.

3. *Maclure, William.*

   Opinions on various subjects. New Harmony, 1831. pp. 640.

4. *Owen, Robert.*

   Life of Robert Owen. Written by himself. London, 1857. Two volumes. pp. 390 and 358.

5. *Owen, Robert Dale.*

   Threading my way: twenty-seven years of autobiography. New York and London, 1874. pp. 360.

6. [*Packard, Frederick Adolphus*].

   Life of Robert Owen. Philadelphia, 1866. pp. 264.

7. *Wood*, C. H.

   First disciple of Pestalozzi. *Indiana School Journal*, November 1892. Vol. 37. pp. 659-665.

8. [*Woodbridge, William Channing*].

Mr. Owen's school at New Harmony. *American Journal of Education*, June 1826, Vol. 1.   pp. 377-378.

VII   PESTALOZZIANISM IN NEW ENGLAND.

1. *Alcott, Amos Bronson.*

Primary education: an account of the method of instruction in primary school No. 1 of Cheshire, Connecticut. *American Journal of Education*, January and February, 1827.   Vol. 3.   pp. 26-31 and 86-94.

2. *Alcott, William A.*

William Channing Woodbridge. *Barnard's American Journal of Education*, 1858. Vol. 5.   pp. 51-64.

3. *Barnard, Henry.*

A chapter in the history of normal schools in New England. *Barnard's American Journal of Education*, 1856. Vol 1.   pp. 587-592.

4. *Barnard, Henry.*

Educational labors of Lowell Mason. *Barnard's American Journal of Education*, 1858. Vol. 4. pp. 141-148.

5. *Barnard, Henry.*

James G. Carter. *Barnard's American Journal of Education*, 1858. Vol. 5. pp. 407-416.

6. *Barnard, Henry.*

William Russell, editor of the first series of the American Journal of Education. *Barnard's American Journal of Education‘* 1857. Vol. 3. pp. 139-146.

7. *Boutwell, George Sewell.*

Pestalozzian system. *Popular Science Monthly*, November 1893. Vol. 44. pp. 55-56.

8. *Fowle, William Bentley.*

Vocal music. *American Annals of Education*, May 1835. Vol. 5. pp. 225-229

9. *Mason, William.*

Memories of a musical life. New York, 1901. pp. 275-290.

10. *Mathews, William Smythe Babcock.*

A hundred years of music in America. Philadelphia, 1900. pp. 34-44.

11. *Monroe, Will Seymour.*

Educational labors of Henry Barnard: a study in the history of American pedagogy. Syracuse, 1893. pp. 35.

12. *Peabody, Elizabeth Palmer.*

Record of Mr. Alcott's school exemplifying the principles and methods of moral culture. Boston, 1874. Third edition. pp. 297.

13. *Sanborn, Franklin Benjamin.*

A. Bronson Alcott: a memoir. *Barnard's American Journal of Education,* 1877. Vol. 27. pp. 225-236.

14. *Sanborn, Franklin Benjamin* and *Harris, William Torrey.*

A. Bronson Alcott: his life and philosophy. Boston, 1893. Two volumes. pp. 679.

15. *Semi-centennial* and other exercises of the state normal school at Westfield, Mass. Boston, 1889. pp. 79.

16. *Winship, Albert Edward.*

Great American educators, with chapters on American education. New York,[1900]. pp. 101-114.

17. *Woodbridge, William Channing.*

On vocal music. American Institute of Instruction for 1830. pp. 233-255.

VIII Pestalozzianism at the Oswego Normal School.

1. *Aber, William M.*

Oswego normal school. *Popular Science Monthly*, May 1893. Vol. 43. pp. 51-76.

2. *Calkins, Norman Allison.*

History of object teaching. *Barnard's American Journal of Education*, 1863. Vol. 12. pp. 633-645.

3. *Gordy, J. P.*

Rise and growth of the normal school idea

in the United States.   Washington, 1891.
pp. 61-75.

4. *Greene, Samuel Stillman.*

Object teaching: its general principles and
the Oswego system.   Proc. National Teachers' Association for 1865.   pp. 245-270.

5. *Historical* sketches relating to the first
quarter century of the state normal and
training school at Oswego, N. Y. Oswego,
1888.   pp. 303.

6. *Hollis, Andrew Phillip.*

Contribution of the Oswego normal school
to educational progress in the United
States.   Boston, 1898.   pp. 128.

7. *Jones, M. E. M.*

Laws of childhood.   *Barnard's American
Journal of Education*, 1863.   Vol. 12.   pp.
629-632.

8. *Monroe, Will Seymour.*

Herman Krüsi, an American Pestalozzian.
Journal of Education (Boston) November
5th, 1903.   Vol. 53.   pp. 304-305.

9. *Monroe, Will Seymour.*

   Memoir of Professor Mary Sheldon Barnes. *Journal of Education* (Boston), September 15th, 1898. Vol. 48. p. 175.

10. *Phelps, William Franklin, et. al.*

    Primary instruction by object lessons: report of the committee of the primary schools of Oswego. *Barnard's American Journal of Education,* 1863. Vol. 12. pp. 605-628.

11. *Sheldon, Edward Austin.*

    Object teaching. *Barnard's American Journal of Education,* 1864. Vol 14. pp. 93-102.

12. *Wilbur, Harvey Backus.*

    Object system of instruction as pursued in the schools of Oswego. *Barnard's American Journal of Education,* 1865. Vol. 15 pp. 189-208.

13. *Winship, Albert Edward.*

    Great American educators, with chapters

on American education.   New York [1900]
pp.   145-161.

IX   WILLIAM T. HARRIS AND PESTALOZZIANISM
IN SCHOOLS OF ST. LOUIS.

1. *Barnard, Henry.*

William Torrey Harris and St. Louis public
schools. *Barnard's American Journal of
Education* 1880.   Vol. 30.   pp. 625-640.

2. *de Guimps, Roger.*

Pestalozzi: his life and work. Translated
by John Russell with an introduction by
R. H. Quick [and an editor's preface by
William T. Harris].   New York, 1897.   pp.
438.

3. *Harris, William Torrey.*

Course of study in the district schools.
Fourteenth annual report of the board of
directors of the St. Louis public schools.
St. Louis, 1869.   pp. 88-98.

4. *Harris, William Torrey.*

Herbert and Pestalozzi compared. *Edu-*

cational Review, May 1893. Vol. 5. pp. 417-423.

5. *Harris, William Torrey.*

How to teach natural sciences in public schools. Syracuse, 1895. Second edition. pp. 46.

X PESTALOZZIAN LITERATURE IN THE UNITED STATES.

1. *Barnard, Henry, editor.*

Pestalozzi and Pestalozzianism. New York, 1859. Two parts. pp. 238 and 230. The same, enlarged under the title Pesta- lozzi and his educational system. Syra- cuse, 1906. pp. 745.*

2. *Biber, E.*

Life and trials of Pestalozzi [Greenbank's Periodical Library]. Philadelphia, 1833.

3. *de Guimps, Roger.*

Pestalozzi; his aim and work. Trans- lated by Margaret Cuthbertson Crombie. Syracuse, 1889. pp. 320. The same,

*See foot note on page 210.

translated by John Russell, New York,
1897, pp. 438.

4. *Krüsi, Herman, Jr.*

Pestalozzi; his life, work, and influence.
New York, [1875]. pp. 248.

5. *Maclure, William.*

An epitome of the improved Pestalozzian
system of education. *American Journal
of Science and Arts*, February 1826, Vol
10. pp. 145-156.

6. *Monroe, Will Seymour.*

Pestalozzian literature in America. *Kindergarten Magazine*, May, 1894, Vol. 6. pp.
673-676.

7. *Pestalozzi.*

Leonard and Gertrude. Translated and
abridged by Eva Channing, with an introduction by G. Stanley Hall. Boston, 1888.
pp. 181.

8. *Pestalozzi.*

How Gertrude teaches her children. Translated by Lucy E. Holland and Frances E.

Turner; and edited, with introduction and notes, by Ebenezer Cooke. Syracuse, 1894 pp. 256.

9. *Pestalozzi.*

Letters on early education, addressed to J. P. Greaves, Esq., Boston, 1830. Same, Syracuse, 1898. pp. 180.

10. *Pinloche, A.*

Pestalozzi and the foundation of the modern elementary school. New York, 1901. pp. 306.

11. *von Raumer, Karl.*

Pestalozzi and Pestalozzianism. Edited by Henry Barnard. Part one: Memoir of Pestalozzi, and biographical sketches of several of his assistants and disciples. pp. 238. Part two: Selections from the publications of Pestalozzi. pp. 230. New York, 1859.] Now published at Syracuse, N. Y.]

INDEX